filthy

filthy

The Weird World of John Waters

By Robrt L. Pela

alyson books
los angeles | new york

MANUFACTURED IN THE UNITED STATES OF AMERICA.

THIS TRADE PAPERBACK ORIGINAL IS PUBLISHED BY
ALYSON PUBLICATIONS,
P.O. BOX 4371, LOS ANGELES, CALIFORNIA 90078-4371.
DISTRIBUTION IN THE UNITED KINGDOM
BY TURNAROUND PUBLISHER SERVICES LTD.,
UNIT 3, OLYMPIA TRADING ESTATE, COBURG ROAD, WOOD GREEN,
LONDON N22 6TZ ENGLAND.

FIRST EDITION: JUNE 2002

02 03 04 05 06 **a** 10 9 8 7 6 5 4 3 2 1

ISBN 1-55583-625-9

CREDITS
COVER DESIGN BY MATT SAMS.
COVER IMAGE PAINTED BY PAUL WILSON. COURTESY ROBRT L. PELA.
INTERIOR ILLUSTRATIONS BY PAUL WILSON.

For Tevye

CONTENTS

Acknowledgments

Endless thanks to John Waters for making such unusual films, to all those quoted herein who made the time to talk to me, and to the amazing Todd Grossman for everything else. Eternal gratitude to my gracious editor, Scott Brassart, who suggested I write a book about his favorite filmmaker; my parents, who are probably horrified; Jennifer Warnes, who sang to me, offered advice, and sent cookies; Michael Thomas Ford, who listened to me whine; James "Beefbob" Zubko, who showed me my first Waters film; the remarkable Joe Blevins, whose insights into John Waters' career are unparalleled; and Cydney "Slimy Cydney the Dehydrated Kidney" Holt Tholl, who many years ago demanded that I become a writer.

I cannot live without Dan Cullinane, Ruth Beaumont, Kim Blake, the lovely Paul Braun, Dominick Abatemarco, Kristi Dempsey, Lisa Sutton, Kate Nolan, Patti Epler, Blake dePastino, David Kalmansohn, and Anne Stockwell.

For assistance and stimulation, thanks to Ron Kraft, Christopher Busa, Lisa Fineberg Malone, Bill Mann, Tom Taylor, David Ruben, Arthur Roger, Matt Sams, Trudy Ring, Ann Moses, and the folks at Movies on Central, Phoenix.

For priceless advice, I'm indebted to Jed Mattes, Tim Miller, Felice Picano, Boze Hadleigh, and Matthew Rettenmund.

I'm grateful to my sixth-grade writing teacher, Mrs. Newville, who in 1974 scribbled in my composition book, "I'm sure you know there are certain subjects that are inappropriate to write about," a note I cherish and have clearly ignored.

And I'm indebted to the extraordinary Paul Wilson, who accidentally inspired this book's title and provided both the cover painting and an introduction to my charming boyfriend.

Finally, I drop a curtsy before Gerry Kroll, a lovely gentleman who long ago gave me my first real writing job and who continues to encourage and inspire me.

Chapter One
THE SKY IS FALLING

"I THINK WHAT INFLUENCES YOU IS MOVIES THAT YOU INNOCENTLY SEE THAT MAKE YOU CRAZY IN A WONDERFUL WAY."

—John Waters

Tiny John Waters, trapped in the body of a 5-year-old, was in a sour mood. He was running out of ways to shake off the tedium of 1951 upper-middle-class suburban Baltimore, and the pressure was starting to get to him. He was afraid he might snap.

He had to escape, and he knew just where he was headed

once he busted out: the "other world," the one he knew about from books and movies and records, which was much more fun than the suburban hell he'd been made to endure. In his story-book *The Little Red Hen,* the sky kept threatening to crash down on a retarded chicken with the amusing name of Henny Penny. In the movies, the Evil Queen wore a creepy black unitard, had a talking mirror, and plotted ways to kill sniffy Snow White for being pretty. Even people who lived in records had it better than him: On his 78 rpm of *Cinderella,* the bitchy Wicked Stepmother got to holler and throw buckets of dirty water on people. Plus she had her own scary theme song (Da-*dada*...Da-*dada*...) that announced her every arrival. For the rest of his life, he wanted that music to play whenever he entered a room.

But that would probably never happen. John was stuck in Baltimore while everybody in the *other* world was having fun. Dorothy was hanging around with Munchkins and ugly flying monkeys; Hansel and Gretel were getting eaten by a hag. But he had to go to church and be nice to other people, even if they were stupid or wore ugly shoes. It wasn't fair. He wanted someone he knew to get their hands chopped off and baked in a pie; instead, he got cheerful neighbors and meat loaf. Goddamn it to hell!

Reading helped, a little. His favorite book was *Slovenly Peter: Cheerful Stories and Funny Pictures for Good Little Folks,* about a bunch of kids who get tortured and die horrible deaths. Like Pauline, who burned herself up playing with matches. Or the kid whose mother had his thumbs cut off because he wouldn't stop sucking them. And the best story of all was about some nasty little boys who make fun of a Negro, so Santa Claus turns them black.

John felt better whenever he played Car Accident. He'd smash up his toy cars, then make up stories about the people trapped inside: They almost always ended up covered in blood and screaming, and someone usually shouted, "Oh, my God, there's been a terrible accident!" Now, *that* was living!

2

But it wasn't enough. Something had to give. He worried that if something exciting didn't happen pretty quickly, he might go nuts, like the Wicked Witch from *The Wizard of Oz*. He was afraid he might *do* something. He liked his family and he didn't want to hurt them, but hey, he was *bored*.

John got up from his desk, where he'd been drawing an electric chair, and went looking for his mother. He found her sitting by the fire, reading *Collier's*. He waited until she looked up from her magazine, and then he just plain blurted it out.

"Mother," he said, "*Please* take me to the junkyard!"

"What to do if your kid is obsessed with car accidents was not in the Dr. Spock book," John Waters recalled many years later. "So she did what any good mother would do: She took me to the junkyard to see the smashed-up cars."

In the half century since that trip to the local dump, Waters has arrived and taken up residence in the other world he dreamed of as a kid—the one filled with demented children and lunatic chickens and mean women who have their own theme music. The sky has been falling for decades, and John Waters is deliriously happy.

As writer and director of more than a dozen infamous film comedies, Waters has redefined the limits of bad taste. His movie heroes have eaten dog shit, injected liquid eyeliner into their veins, and been raped by giant lobsters. His early acting troupe, mostly unknowns whose primary talents were their odd looks or willingness to act perverted on screen, became superstars after appearing in his films. He discovered Divine, Ricki Lake, and Mink Stole; revived the careers of Tab Hunter, Pia Zadora, and Deborah Harry; and influenced hundreds of outsider artists to pursue high-profile careers. His early films, which draw on his personal obsessions, made filth fashionable, and the popularity of his later, Hollywood-produced movies placed him among the most recognized directors working in American cinema today. Waters' wacko plotlines and innovative casting have made a lasting impact on pop culture and have earned him the title "The Prince of Puke."

It certainly wasn't what his parents had in mind for their eldest son. John Sr., owner of a company that sold fire protection equipment, hoped young John would take over the family business one day; mom Patricia presumed her Johnny would marry a nice girl from Baltimore and raise a houseful of grandchildren. Neither imagined that their firstborn would grow up to make movies in which their neighbors' children ate puke or masturbated with the business end of a rosary.

Yet Mr. and Mrs. Waters unintentionally kick-started the showbiz obsession that eventually led to such stunning imagery. Without meaning to, they opened the door to the other world their son longed to live in when they took him to a broadcast of his favorite television program, *The Howdy Doody Show,* in New York when he was just 7 years old.

Waters had been infatuated with the antics of *Howdy* host Buffalo Bob and his degenerate pals for as long as he could remember. Clarabell the Clown was his favorite: A man with a woman's name, Clarabell was scary and funny at the same time. He wore clown white and acted retarded, and he and Bob hung around in a vaguely magical place where grown-ups talked to marionettes and dressed like children. No one had boring jobs or seemed to care about much more than the next cartoon or the names of the kids visiting the Peanut Gallery, which is what Bob called his studio audience.

Waters' visit to the Peanut Gallery in 1953 changed his opinion about the true nature of show-business magic and irrevocably altered the course of his little life.

"I saw there were five Howdy Doody puppets and 10 cameras and that the stage was tiny," he remembered many years later. "I couldn't even see the puppets, and Buffalo Bob was mean to me.

But still I thought, *This is all a lie, and this is what I want to do forever.* And I knew then I was gonna be in show business."

Before that, Waters had contented himself with violent childhood fantasies. Obsessed with amusement park rides, he'd daydreamed about roller coasters that jumped their tracks and crushed crowds of innocent bystanders waiting in line for cotton candy. He'd spent hours drawing a carnival ride called the Crush, a modified Ferris wheel whose patrons were strapped into their seats and then slowly ground to death.

Other days, he'd pretended to be other people, dressing up as the Wicked Witch from *The Wizard of Oz* or as his other favorite villain, Captain Hook. Taping his father's neckties to his forehead and shoving a coat hanger hook up his sleeve, he'd stalk the neighborhood, glowering at people and shouting dialogue from *Peter Pan:* "Quiet, you scugs! Or I'll cast anchor with ye!"

But after seeing Clarabell out of costume, little John figured he could be a big fake just as easily as some middle-aged, overweight guy in a clown suit. Suddenly, he had a goal: He was headed for showbiz, where he would rub elbows with all the weirdos he saw in movies and on television.

Waters turned the family garage into a haunted house, charging neighborhood kids admission to be scared by blasts of cold air and spooky noises. But his first attempt at entertaining the public was a flop: Local parents forbade their children to return to his horror house, and with no audience, he was forced to abandon the game.

His next show business venture proved more successful. After seeing the 1953 Leslie Caron feature *Lili,* which featured a lot of ornate puppetry, Waters began staging his own puppet shows. For $20, Baltimore housewives could hire 7-year-old John's violent version of Punch and Judy (in which both puppets got eaten by a dragon) for their children's birthday parties. Despite the gratuitous gore or perhaps because of it, Waters' programs were in constant demand. He did as many as five shows a week and brought home pots of money. When he grew bored with his scripts, which he wrote by hand on lined paper, he'd terrorize the audience by chasing after them with the dragon puppet.

Today, Patricia Waters prefers to believe that the puppets in *Lili* had the biggest impact on her son's later film career, but in reality young John had found a greater influence.

"I could see the local drive-in by climbing up on top of this nearby construction site," Waters says. "I would take binoculars and go up to the top of this site and watch bad movies."

He was especially taken with the tacky films of director William Castle, whose shameless screen gimmicks with names like "Illusion-O" and "Emergo," an effect that sent a skeleton out over the audience on a wire (in *House on Haunted Hill*), were more memorable than the movies in which they appeared. Waters especially loved *The Tingler,* a Castle movie that featured an effect called "Percepto," where theater seats were wired to give mild electric shocks at opportune moments of suspense.

Waters began working references to Castle's cheapjack pictures into his puppet shows. He even staged a puppet version of *The Tingler,* with younger brother Steve stationed under the benches at kiddie parties, grabbing ankles during key moments in the story. But *The Tingler* didn't scare the local cake-and-ice-cream crowd so much as confuse them, and word began to spread among Baltimore housewives that Johnny Waters was getting a little weird.

"It was about then I realized I'd better get another job," Waters says. "It was really uncool to be doing puppet shows for money, anyway. I never told anyone I was doing it."

Waters was anxious to grow up. "I couldn't wait to be a teenager so I could get pimples," he wrote in *Shock Value,* a collection of autobiographical essays. "When I entered junior high, I received the thrill of my life: Actual girl juvenile delinquents were in my class, and to my astonishment, they got into catfights. I immediately lost interest in the school's curriculum and concentrated completely on every move of these cheap girls."

His female classmates, who painted their lips with pimple medicine and refused to do their homework, became an obsession. Their teased hair, huge vinyl purses, and sour attitudes exemplified the rock-and-roll juvenile delinquent stance that Waters aspired to. When the scarier "skagettes" began to drop out or were expelled, he invented his own, sketching them in his notebook and writing long, elaborate life stories filled with sorrow, switchblades, and teenage pregnancy.

When he wasn't drawing delinquent girls, Waters was at the movies. "The drive-in was my temple," he says. "I went to the drive-in literally every night, because it was the only place where you could go unsupervised. Those drive-in years are where my film knowledge came from, in one sense—all the exploitation movies."

He usually went with lifelong friend Mary Vivian Pearce, whom Waters has always called Bonnie. He says her influence resonates in every one of his pictures. "There are lots of things in all my movies that come from growing up with Bonnie," he says. "She's the only one of all the people from back then who is in all of my movies."

The Pearces were family friends, and Waters had known Bonnie his whole life. The teenagers began to spend more time together, and always ended up in trouble. "We were always getting thrown out of CYO dances or hooking school," Pearce says. "We were juvenile delinquents."

Waters remembers, "I lived at my parents' and she lived at her parents'. The quickest way for us to meet was walking up the railroad tracks. So we'd both walk up these railroad tracks and see each other in the distance. It was very Tennessee Williams."

The teens were forbidden by their parents to see one another, so Pearce would arrange dates with local boys, ditching them as soon as they left her parents' house. She'd meet up with Waters, usually in the worst dives in downtown Baltimore, and the pair would spend the evening drinking and crashing parties, where they'd dance the Bodie Green, a vulgar bump-and-grind they'd perfected.

Waters has written, "Parents should worry if their children haven't been arrested by the time they turn 16." But he managed to make it to that age without being tossed in jail. He was enrolled in a Christian Brothers high school, where he disrupted class by laughing at the preposterously pious lessons. He remembers being attacked one day by his religion teacher for laughing at the notion of manna from heaven. When Waters guffawed, "Oh, sure, I can hear the weather report now: partly cloudy with brief showers of bread," his instructor pounced on him.

It's no wonder Waters frequently played hooky. He'd hitchhike downtown and convince young women ("I soon learned that hairdressers were the best") to phone the school and pose as his mother calling to say he'd be absent that day. Then he'd spend the day at the movies, watching the films his Sunday school teachers forbade him to see.

"The nuns at Catholic Sunday school initially interested me in forbidden films," he says, "and I thank God for pointing me toward my vocation so early in life."

When he did attend school, the other students mostly ignored him. "I was never very close with my fellow classmates. My real friends were from my own neighborhood and wanted to be just as rotten as I did." Small and odd-looking, John sported a bleached-orange forelock and flamboyant clothing. He dodged hazing from local bullies by making them laugh and posing as a rebel. "The bullies wouldn't beat you up if they knew you were against authority," he says.

Waters began using drugs as a high school senior when a member of the student council offered him a joint. He quickly turned his neighborhood friends on to pot; soon after, the group discovered LSD and was tripping regularly.

That group had grown to include Mona Montgomery, a high

school freshman so notorious for fashion crimes and hooking class that she was suspended from the entire Baltimore County school system. (Mona Montgomery is not her real name. Waters explained to *Provincetown Arts* writer Gerald Peary in 1998, "I changed her name in my book *Shock Value* because I don't know where she is today. She's not in show business and she's not a public figure.")

Mona and Waters became a crack shoplifting team, stealing records and art prints and anything else that wasn't nailed down from local department stores. The pair often hitchhiked together to New York City, where they did drugs and panhandled movie money. They watched films that weren't being screened anywhere else in mid-'60s America: trash-art epics by Kenneth Anger and the Kuchar brothers, and experimental movies by a new artist named Andy Warhol.

"These were the people who made me want to make movies," Waters says today. "I saw everything they did, and those movies were the biggest influence on me up to that point in my life."

Back in Baltimore, John Waters was anxious to put those influences to use. He had just been given his first movie camera: a small, hand-held 8mm Brownie, a gift from his grandmother on his 17th birthday. Armed with a camera, some film that Mona had shoplifted, and an enormous amount of chutzpah, John Waters was ready to make his first picture. And he was about to meet his muse.

Chapter Two
ONE DAY IN BUMBERG

"If I had to live in Baltimore 52 weeks of the year, I'd go out of my mind."

—John Waters

My name is Robrt Pela. I've been in Baltimore for an entire day and no one has called me "Hon." I'm very disappointed.

I've come here in search of the Baltimore of John Waters' movies, the place where everyone is a grumpy housewife with a beehive or a drunken delinquent or a slovenly drag queen with a bad temper. I'm looking for the Baltimore that Waters has written about, the one populated exclusively by mean hillbillies, where overopinionated, narrow-minded, politically incorrect, aggressively stupid people shout at you for no apparent reason.

I'm convinced—after a day of junk shops and crab cakes and dogging a dozen sites from *Pecker*—that the place that Waters calls the Hairdo Capital of the World exists only in his mind. The town itself is certainly strange, full of weird museums and oddball monuments. And some of the folks I've met speak with the same indescribable, mush-mouthed accent as Waters' people. But no one's thrown a mackerel at me. No snaggle-toothed punk has accosted me, demanding money at knifepoint. Even in the worst part of town—the filthy inner city, where I wandered among decaying row houses in search of angry reprobates—people were shockingly ordinary, even kind.

I've decided, on the morning of my second day in Charm City, that I need to head for Waters' favorite spots, places I'd dismissed yesterday as being too obvious. On my way, I stop at a convenience store in Cockeysville and ask a stock boy where they keep the mineral water. I'm hoping he'll laugh at me or throw me out of the store for being highfalutin, but he just smiles and says, "Sawn eauver bah the Cake." ("It's on over by the Coke."). I can't win.

So I decide to board a bus—where better to meet scary weirdos?—until I notice that all the bus stop benches bear bookish slogans: "Baltimore, the City That Reads" or "Official Reading Spot." I hail a cab instead.

I head first for Atomic Books, a shop revered by Waters fans as the very best place to find the sort of stuff that, well, Waters fans love: underground books, fanzines, adult comics, typo-plagued Asian movie mags, Highway Safety Victim videos, *Flying Nun* lunch boxes, Jesus refrigerator magnets, Columbine High School paraphernalia, and other offbeat and hard-core junk. (Atomic's slogan is "Literary Finds for Mutated Minds," and Waters himself has referred to the place as providing "a reading list from hell.")

I'm hoping to overhear a couple of perverts discussing the latest issue of *Murder Can Be Fun* or to see a fight break out between two trailer-park punks, but Baltimore's famously alternative bookstore is surprisingly calm. At the magazine rack, where each title is at least vaguely naughty, I flip through copies of *Bondage Gallery* and *Adult Video News*. When I try to chat up a blue-haired girl who's reading a back issue of *The Dana Plato News Digest,* she gives me a tight smile and flees.

After my next couple of attempts to make friends fail (I thought nerdy inverts *liked* talking to strangers), I head for the checkout line. My loot includes a copy of *The Adult Baby Catalog,* a lavishly illustrated celebration of infantilism that features color photographs of grown women in giant diapers and middle-aged men in dirndls and Heidi braids. I've also found an Infant of

Prague night-light and a first edition of *The Hairdo Handbook*, an astonishingly expensive 1960s hardcover about how to rat your wig into big ugly torpedo shapes.

At the checkout, a sign explains that Big Geeky Brother is watching me. In the spirit of voyeurism, the store's twisted Atomic Cam broadcasts freeze-framed photos of customers onto Atomic's whacked-out Web site. I'm a little unnerved to discover that any asshole in Toledo with a Web-wired computer could have been watching me peruse the latest issue of *The Patty Duke Fanzine*.

"Take a picture, it'll last longer!" I snarl at the clerk for no reason except that I'm hoping to incite a sour exchange with a Baltimoron. Instead, the much-tattooed youth merely points to a hand-lettered sign explaining that photographs of unruly customers (and anyone who bounces a check) are posted on the Web site's "Official Atomic Shit List."

I cover my face as I exit.

Next door, I stumble into the American Dime Museum, a dusty row house crowded with circus and sideshow oddities. Baltimore has a lightbulb museum, a dentistry museum, and a museum dedicated to *Star Wars* toys, but the American Dime Museum is the one that John Waters has personally endorsed by serving on its board of directors. Admission to Baltimore's equivalent of the Smithsonian costs me 30 dimes, but I figure I'm certain to bump into weirdos *here*.

Instead, I see the skeleton of a 10-foot-tall Peruvian Amazon, a maraschino cherry bottle containing a deformed human fetus, and the corpse of the Samoan Sea Worm—a surly, mummified mermaid whose diet consisted of kittens and the occasional sailor. The usual sideshow stuff—two-headed goats, a pickled pig fetus, a handful of shrunken heads—is displayed alongside a glass jar containing a huge, lumpy mass of chewed gum removed from the stomach of a local artist, a dented can of beef ravioli, and "The World's Largest—and Only—Ball o' Ties."

Downstairs, there's the Rangoon Sewer Serpent, a fierce, toothy ass-biter that once plagued the water closets of East Asia, and Fivey, a taxidermied five-legged beagle. My favorite exhibit is the Lincoln Coprolite, supposedly the last piece of excrement pinched off by the 16th president of the United States, retrieved shortly after his death from a privy at Ford's Theatre.

It's clear to me that a lot of this stuff is bogus, like the obviously phony Hand of Spider Lillie, a shrivel of twisted beef jerky sporting a secret-compartment ring from which Lillie, an Australian whore, released poisonous spiders into her tricks' hair. Another fraudulent attraction, the Minotaur, is a man-size mummified head with a pair of deer's antlers glued onto it. Its ears are a pair of dog chews.

Standing near the nasty remains of yet another mythological reptile, I spot a crabby-looking teen wearing a "Divine Rules!" T-shirt. I point to her shirt and, hoping to sound like a dopey tourist, say, "Hey, is that Divine?" The girl rolls her eyes and says, "No, it's Ann-Margret."

At last, I think to myself, *a grumpy Baltimorean.* I ask the girl her name and she scowls at me. "I'm sorry, I don't talk to fags," she says.

Jackpot! I screw up my face and spit back, "Yeah, and I don't talk to assholes, asshole!" The girl begins giggling and throws her arms around me.

"Finally," she yells into my left armpit, "a mean Baltimore guy!" She pulls away and calls out over her shoulder, "Hey, Tina! Come here! I finally met a bitchy Baltimore fag!"

The girl, who introduces herself as Misty, explains that she and her friend drove all the way here from Cleveland, hoping to see some of the Baltimore they've come to love from John Waters' films.

"I'm the biggest Divine fan in the world," Misty promises, "and we've been here for two days and we just haven't met *any* trashy people. We've been walking around in all the scariest parts of town, and everyone we've met has been so normal. Until now," she adds happily.

When I tell Misty that I too am from Ohio and am looking for the same Baltimore that she's after, she lets out a sigh. Tina arrives and Misty tells her, "Sorry. It's just another douche bag from the Midwest."

I leave then and head over to Flashback, a junk shop owned by Bob Adams, a former Dreamlander and Waters' good friend. In a previous life, the shop housed Edith's Shopping Bag, a notorious and popular thrift store owned by Edith Massey.

Bob is very friendly and very busy grousing at a handsome clerk named Dominic who's supposed to be pricing tchotchkes but is instead talking to tourists. I want to ask Bob about where to go to meet scary white trash with greasy hair, but he's preoccupied, posing for photographs with a couple of John Waters fans who have brought him a giant pretzel. I buy a ceramic plate bearing the slogan "Welcome to Charm City!" and an Edith Massey greeting card. As I'm leaving, Bob's new friends are reciting his dialogue from *Pink Flamingos* to him.

Up the street at a boutique called Killer Trash, I speak with the owner, Elaine, who tells me she appeared in *Serial Mom* and "knows all John's friends real good." That night, she says, she's going to Susan Lowe's birthday party, where she's sure to see plenty of hair hoppers.

"The really trashy people in John's movies are *very* real," Elaine tells me in a spongy Baltimore accent. "You just gotta know where to look is all." I hang out for another half an hour, but Elaine never once calls me Hon.

My friend Tom Taylor says Elaine is wrong. The cheap girls and vulgar hippies in Waters' films are just exaggerated stereotypes, he says. "John is fixated on East Side white trash, and he gives the impression that everyone here is like that. We're not. And most of those trashy people aren't that weird or wild either."

Later that day, Tom, who grew up in Baltimore and went to

school with Mink Stole ("I knew her when her name was still Nancy!") offers to help me find John Waters' Baltimore. I suggest we go someplace where we can watch teabagging, but Tom just laughs at me. Instead, we visit the sub shop from *Pecker,* the Marbles' house from *Pink Flamingos,* and the infamous statue of George Washington's hard-on. (Sure enough, viewed from the east, George's outstretched arm looks like a giant, erect penis.)

We drive around looking in vain for a pit beef stand and finally settle for eating crab cakes in a creepy bar. Later we stop at Divine's grave, which is covered in lipstick marks and messages written in makeup. Someone has draped a black pleather jacket with a swastika painted on it over the gravestone. Tom and I watch while two fans leave love notes to Divine in a little hole in the ground next to her grave, which makes us want to leave in a hurry.

Tom drops me at my motel, a filthy Econo Lodge in Cockeysville, and I drive myself over to the Charles Theater, John Waters' favorite childhood movie house. *Cecil B. Demented* is showing. I buy a ticket from a churlish teen with several face piercings and a bag of greasy popcorn from a slutty-looking bald girl at the concession stand. All the kids who work at the Charles look like the Sprocket Holes, the demented young punks in *Cecil.*

The theater is mostly empty, and everyone there seems more excited by *Cecil*'s scenery ("Look! There's my dry cleaner's!") than by the film itself. I've seen the movie before, so I spend most of my time eavesdropping on the elderly couple in front of me, who talk throughout the picture. They seem to be having an argument about cocktail onions.

After the film, I walk to a seedy bar, where I drink Glenlivet and read Mink Stole's advice column in *City Paper,* Baltimore's alternative weekly. I confess to my waitress that I am one of those assholes who come to Baltimore expecting to run into the cast of *Multiple Maniacs,* and she shakes her head and smiles, as if to say, "I've heard *that* one before." While she's telling me about the guy who came in claiming to be Spiro Agnew, I spot a familiar face at the next table.

It takes me a moment to place Mary Vivian Pearce, in part because she looks so *different*. For one thing, her hair is darker and very short, and even from several yards away in bad bar light, she looks, well, *older*. I feel stupid staring at her, but I can't believe my good fortune. I watch her awhile and realize that the kids at the table behind me are staring at her too. I resort to stealing glances at her instead.

Just after last call, Mary Vivian heads for the door, and I follow her. I'm not sure what I'm going to say to her—"I'm sorry for staring"? "How come you're not blond anymore"?—but I never get a chance to find out. Outside, I'm accosted by an ugly punk who grabs my arm and shoves a flier into the waistband of my pants. He's shouting something about a band called the Spineless Kitten People. His breath smells like curdled milk, and he's missing his two front teeth. By the time I pull away from him, Mary Vivian has climbed onto a rickety bicycle and is pedaling away.

As I'm standing there, watching her go, someone shoves me from behind. I turn to find another surly youth, this one with a fluorescent Mohawk and a spike through his nose. "Hey, you stupid fucking asshole!" he screams, in a truly terrifying Baltimore accent. "What the fuck are you starin' at? Ain't you never seen a chick ridin' a bike before?"

The young man is clearly shit-faced. While he continues his rant—"I fuckin' hate seein' stupid people standin' around starin' at fuckin' other people who're just mindin' their own damn business on their own damn bikes for fuck's sake!"—a miniskirted teen with a towering green hairdo approaches me.

I'm convinced she's about to start screaming too, but instead she places her hand on my arm and says, gently, "It's OK. He don't mean nothin'. He just got outta jail, and he's mad cuz he caught his girl shackin' up with his dad." While I'm trying to think of something to say, the young woman is guiding me back toward the door of the bar. "You just go on back inside and get yourself a nice big drink," she says, and then she pats my hand and says, "Go on inside, Hon."

Instead, I return to Cockeysville and pack my bags.

Chapter Three
DIVINE INTERVENTION

"I CAN'T HELP IT. I ENJOY THE COMPANY OF MURDERERS, RAPISTS, AND CHILD MOLESTERS."

—John Waters

"I first noticed him waiting for the school bus," John Waters says of Divine. "He lived right up the street from our house, so in a sense, he really was the girl next door."

Divine, then known as Glenn Milstead, was pretty hard to miss. Obese and enormously effeminate, he stood out among the other "county kids."

"He was anything but flamboyant," Waters recalls. "He tried to be normal and fit in, but he got hassled and beaten up every day by other kids. Because, you know, he held his books like a girl. He would just be waiting for the bus, this creature with dyed red hair, and I would see my father shudder. For no reason! I thought, 'How great! He can make my father angry just waiting for a bus.'"

Glenn was a close friend of Carol Wernig, who lived across the street from the Milsteads. Wernig's own extreme sense of fashion had caught Waters' attention some time before; he'd later credit her with changing his life.

"I was immediately drawn to her bleached white bubble hair-do, turned green from chlorine in swimming pools," he wrote in *Shock Value,* "and to her pimples, which were thickly covered in green medicine."

Wernig introduced him to Glenn, who stunned Waters with his defiantly swishy behavior. "After the immediate shock wore off," Waters says, "I became intrigued by the hostile reactions he got just because he acted like a girl."

Glenn was born Harris Glenn Milstead in the Baltimore sub-urb of Towson, and he and his parents lived for a time in a 28-room estate where F. Scott and Zelda Fitzgerald had lived while Zelda was an outpatient of nearby Sheppard Pratt mental hospi-tal. Young Glenn liked to tell people that Zelda had set fire to the top floor of the house and that he could feel "a presence" upstairs. "My cousins wouldn't go up there when they would come visit," he recalled.

In 1958, 12-year-old Glenn and his parents moved from the Fitzgerald house to nearby Lutherville, where Wernig and Waters lived. The Milsteads' new, less palatial home was just six doors down from the Waters house, but because Glenn went to public school and kept to himself, he and Waters didn't meet until Carol Wernig introduced them.

Although they'd eventually become the Josef von Sternberg and Marlene Dietrich of the underground movement, Divine's first impression of Waters and his pals wasn't a favorable one. "I thought, 'God, what a sleazy crew they are,'" Divine told the *San Francisco Chronicle* shortly before his death in 1988. "Everybody liked living in poverty and filth. No one I knew lived like that. I was stuck in a middle-class mentality."

Waters, on the other hand, was instantly taken with Glenn. "He and Carol used to play cards and gamble for pimple medicine," Waters recalls. "I was looking for a leading lady for my next film and when I saw Divine dancing the Dirty Boogie at a local swim club, I knew I had met my goddess."

Waters eventually renamed his protégé Divine, although not necessarily in honor of the drag queen heroine of Jean Genet's *Our Lady of the Flowers,* which Waters had recently read.

"It didn't come from the Genet book like everybody thinks, although that might have had a subconscious influence that I don't remember. I gave him the name in *Roman Candles,* which was influenced by the Warhol films and that kind of anger. People had those kinds of names in all of those underground films.

"I don't even remember how the name came to me," Waters told *Vanity Fair* in 1988, after Divine's death. "Probably something from my Catholic upbringing. [Divine] looked the word up in the dictionary and seemed satisfied. Yes, he agreed, ever so modestly, he truly was Divine."

Glenn and Carol introduced Waters to David Lochary, a beauty school dropout who constantly changed the color of his long hair—it was silver when he and Waters met—and whose girlfriend, Roxanne, terrified Mrs. Waters with her extreme fashion sense.

Despite his flashy appearance, Mrs. Waters was fond of Lochary, who charmed her with good manners and his fake British accent. "I like David," Mrs. Waters told her son. "He's the only lady you've ever brought home."

Lochary introduced Waters to Pat Moran, who'd recently been divorced and was now whooping it up as a popular fag hag. Moran would eventually become famous as Waters' best friend and the casting director on all his films. But back then she was merely infamous. She and Divine had been the prime suspects when their friend Sally was slain minutes after Moran and Divine left her apartment. Eventually both were cleared, and the murderer, a serial killer, was apprehended.

"Pat and I are like Siamese twins," Waters says of his and Moran's enduring friendship. "Even her longtime husband, Chuck [Yeaton], accepts the fact that I go along with the deal. He even sends me candy for Valentine's Day."

Moran introduced Waters to Maelcum Soul, a local eccentric whose radical makeup and outrageous thrift-store chic had an enormous impact on the look of the young filmmaker's earliest characters. He referred to her as "my first real star" and marveled at her twisted appearance: maroon hair, a dozen pairs of false eyelashes, and Kabuki-white face powder. "She was a woman female impersonator," Waters says.

Soul was a barmaid at Martick's, a downtown Baltimore bar where an odd mix of deadbeats, drag queens, and beatniks mingled. Waters became a regular. He was fascinated with the look of East Baltimore. Its aesthetic—tacky storefronts, rundown row houses, and various lowlifes haunting the streets—would later inform his films.

"It completely fascinated me, because I was raised to look down on that," he says of East Baltimore. "So I looked up to it. Obsessively." Waters' teenage rebellion became a stylized us-versus-them in which upper-middle-class suburbanites were the bad guys. "The villains are always suburbanites who are uptight and don't mind their own business," he has said about his films.

By now, Waters was regularly hooking high school and dropping acid. When he wasn't hanging at Martick's, he hitchhiked to Manhattan with Mona or another of his friends.

"Bonnie and I would take speed and go see three movies a day, and that was our idea of a great day," he remembers.

Waters' grades were so lousy and he'd missed so many classes that the Christian Brothers faculty wouldn't allow him to participate in his high school graduation ceremony. He didn't care; his life centered around drugs and drugged-out weirdos, and he spent most of his time at Martick's or at Divine's numerous "elegant" dinner parties, which were always paid for with credit cards or cash that Divine had stolen from his mother.

Between acid trips, Waters managed to make it through two semesters at the nearby University of Baltimore, and his grades were good enough for him to gain acceptance into New York University's film school.

"I figured that if I was going to be forced to continue this charade of education, I might as well be in Greenwich Village," Waters says. He rarely attended classes; when he did, he was appalled at the pretentious films that students were made to watch. He began spending his days downtown, moving from one tiny movie house to another. "*That's* where my real film education began," he says.

In the early '60s, New York's Lower East Side was home to a burgeoning underground film movement. New American Cinema, as critics tagged it, was home to movie mavericks with no formal training and uncommon, often gloomy visions. The movement was centered around venues like the Gramercy Arts, Bleecker Street, and Charles theaters, and filmmaker Ken Jacobs' Ferry Street loft.

Peopled by dilettantes, beatnik intellectuals, and homosexuals, the decadent underground was light-years away from the uptight classrooms of NYU's film school and from the workaday world of Lutherville. An April 1967 *Playboy* article on experimental film referred to the denizens of underground cinema as "a dreadfully intense bunch of people."

Among them, Waters was in heaven. Here at last were people with whom he could discuss John Rechy novels and Fassbinder films; kids like himself who disdained the dreck that passed for popular cinema. He made friends with people who had similar ideas about life and art and who supported his interest in drugs and movies. And sex. Waters was delighted with the sexual candor of his new pals, many of whom were openly gay and anxious to express their sexuality in their lives and their art.

Film critic Jonas Mekas began to write regularly about the underground in *The Village Voice* and *Film Culture* magazine, covering the work of emerging filmmakers like Andy Warhol, Stan Brakhage, Kenneth Anger, and Jack Smith. Mekas gave special attention to Mike and George Kuchar, twin brothers whose radical short films were special favorites of Waters.

"*They* made me want to make films," he says of the Kuchar brothers. "They were the first people who ever idolized Douglas Sirk; they were so ahead of their time. Their films were shot in very lurid color, and they were, of all the underground filmmakers, the biggest influence on me."

Born in the Bronx in 1942, the Kuchars began making films when they were teenagers. By the time Waters joined the cinema underground, the Kuchars' cult status had been established with such low-budget classics as *I Was a Teenage Rumpot* (1960), *Pussy on a Hot Tin Roof* (1961), and George's infamous *Hold Me While I'm Naked* (1966). The brothers' sexy sci-fi spoof, *Sins of the Fleshapoids* (1965), was Waters' favorite.

"*Sins of the Fleshapoids* was this lurid melodrama," he recalls, "with lurid Douglas Sirk lighting, and a soundtrack stolen from big Hollywood movies, overacting, and garish colors. This meant more to me than all the other underground films. They did it with their friends, like Warhol, only there was more melodrama, which I loved."

When he wasn't watching yet another screening of *Fleshapoids,* Waters was experiencing live theater. He religiously attended plays by Samuel Beckett and LeRoi Jones.

But mostly he went to the movies. Waters watched Warhol's *Couch* (1964), Kenneth Anger's *Scorpio Rising* (1964), and Jean

Genet's first film, *Un Chant d'Amour* (1950) as well as anything that showed at the Cinematheque, the Gate, the Bridge, and St. Mark's Church.

"I hung out with Warhol groupies," he recalls. "We'd drop acid and go to four movies in a row." Water supported his four-film-a-day habit by stealing textbooks from NYU's student bookstore, then reselling them to the store. Attending the university was, Waters admits today, "just an excuse to move to New York. I lived in the dorm and went to movies every day. I got a much better perspective on films than I would have in the classroom."

The idyll was short-lived. Three months into the first semester, Waters was booted out of NYU for drug use. "Seven of us were called into the dean's office and told that they knew we smoked marijuana," he wrote in *Shock Value*, "and that we had to leave immediately; our parents were on the way to get us. We were told to never tell anyone what had happened, and guards were placed outside our dorm rooms so we couldn't flee before our parents arrived."

Anxious to embarrass the school, Waters immediately phoned the New York *Daily News* and squealed. The story received banner headlines the next day ("Pot Bust at NYU") and was included later that same year in Richard Goldstein's book *One in Seven: Drugs on Campus.*

Waters was eager to leave NYU, if not New York City. "You had to go for two years before you got to make a 15-minute short with three other students," he sneered several years later. "I can make movies better just on my own."

He was eager to get started. Inspired by what he'd seen on screens in Manhattan, Waters set about convincing his Baltimore friends that they were movie stars. He knew, from watching Warhol's stable of "superstars," that having a troupe of distinctive players meant he could ape the celebrity culture of Hollywood. "Warhol's influence on me was giving me the confidence that I could make films with my friends, for no money," he says.

Without any kind of a budget, Waters knew he had to create films that made up in style for what they lacked in nearly every other category. He would, he decided, promote recognizable faces and follow the Kuchars' dictum that bad acting was better than non-acting. He'd substitute confrontation for continuity, sleaze and shock for talent.

Waters had already made his first movie: *Hag in a Black Leather Jacket* was shot in 1964 with film that Mona had stolen from her job in a photo supply store. The 15-minute black-and-white short starred Mary Vivian Pearce, Mona, and some of Waters' "boring school acquaintances" and was filmed at his parents' home.

Inspired by the art-house films he admired, *Hag* details the marriage between a white woman and a black man. He courts her by carrying her around in a trash can. The couple is eventually wed in a rooftop ceremony. The wedding is presided over by a Ku Klux Klansman and attended by a jock in drag; other guests are dressed in tinfoil and American flags. The film ends with Bonnie doing the Bodie Green in a cocktail dress "borrowed" from Mrs. Waters. The final shot shows the words "The End," written on a piece of paper, being flushed down the toilet.

One scene is double exposed, an arty touch that Waters swears was accidental. "I put the same roll of film back in the camera," he laughs. "When I saw the footage, I thought, *What's this?*"

Apparently Mr. and Mrs. Waters were good sports about the project. Besides the location and purloined frock, Mrs. Waters provided the piano accompaniment heard on the film's soundtrack. After the film was shot, Waters attempted to get it booked into a local drive-in. "That's how naïve I was," he says. "I didn't know that 8mm movies couldn't be shown there."

The film was screened only once, at a local beatnik coffeehouse. Waters passed a hat afterward. Because the film was stolen and there were no production costs other than developing, the movie broke even. "I made about $30 that night, which is about what the movie cost to make," Waters remembers.

Waters has referred to *Hag* as "terrible" and "mercifully short," and once told an audience at one of his art shows, "That film is in the bottom of my closet, where it belongs." But *Hag in a Black Leather Jacket*—along with Waters' other early short films—is coveted by his fans, few of whom have seen it. The filmmaker contends that even if he wanted to screen the film today, he couldn't.

"The problem is that it's shot in 8mm with the sound on a separate tape," he says. "So you need a reel-to-reel tape recorder to sync the sound with the picture. And it's just not worth the effort, believe me."

Before Waters could shoot his next picture, he'd have to get the armed forces off his back. The NYU staff had recommended to the senior Waters that their son undergo psychiatric treatment, which John agreed to in the hope that it would help him dodge the draft.

"When I finally got my induction papers, I showed them to the shrink and asked him to write me a note to get me out of it. He smiled and said, 'John, I think the Army would be the best thing in the world for you.' I never went back to *that* quack."

Forced to fill out his induction papers in the summer of 1965, Waters played his trump card. "I checked 'bed wetter,' 'gay,' 'junkie,' every little silly thing. I had to go to the shrink there, but he just said, 'What do you like to do in bed?' He was so perverted!"

After a two-hour interview with the psychiatrist, Waters was sent home. But all his efforts to dodge the draft with admissions of personal and sexual quirks were for naught. "At the end of all that, I was one pound too thin," he says. "You had to be 130 and I weighed 129." Several years later, on the set of *Cry-Baby*, Waters and rock icon Iggy Pop, who was appearing in the film, would commiserate about their draft status.

"We both had the same (draft board) classification," Waters says. "We were both 1Y, which basically means after hairdressers they'll take us. I remember when the Gulf War broke out, we both said, 'God, we're 1Y, do you think they'll call us?' They never called *me!*"

Free to continue his civilian life, Waters returned to partying with friends and began scrounging funds for his next film. In between hits of acid, he and Pearce went to work for a door-to-door survey company.

"No one would let me in their house," Waters says, "because I had real long hair and looked weird, so I made up every one of the answers. I had to be so many different people, it was really a good way to develop characters."

While Waters honed his writing skills, Pearce discovered a new way to make money. "Bonnie used to send away for the whole UNICEF kit, and she'd get dressed up really straight and collect money, and we'd buy LSD with it."

During one of their better acid trips, Waters and Mona decided to hitchhike to Provincetown, the penultimate artists' colony at the tip of Cape Cod in Massachusetts. P-town was the perfect place for the young Waters to "find himself" among the gay artistes, hippies, and assorted other fringies who peopled the place.

"I remember getting off Route 6 by the A&P," he says, "and walking up and seeing Commercial Street and thinking, *God, is this cool!*"

When Waters visited the Benches, a local hangout next to Town Hall, he spotted a local rock star with waist-length hair and a hook for a hand, "which is something I always wanted," he says. "I was so impressed. I thought this must be the coolest place I've ever been, although Mona and I didn't know anybody."

Waters ran into Sique Stole, an acquaintance from Baltimore, who showed them the best places to drink and carouse. John and Mona stayed until they ran out of money. And they returned to Provincetown the following summer with Bonnie in tow.

They rented a tiny basement apartment with ceilings so low

that Waters could never stand up straight. The trio threw parties, dropped acid, and made friends with the local riffraff. Mona found work in a dress shop called the Queen of Diamonds, and Waters worked briefly at a boutique across the street called No Fish Today. He was fired when he refused to wait on customers, preferring to read instead. He wanted to work at East End Bookshop, but owner Molly Malone Cook wasn't hiring. Cook liked Waters, though, and finally agreed that he could work in her shop whenever it rained because tourists flocked to the shop on wet days. "So wherever I happened to be, whatever I was doing, when it started raining I had to literally *run* to work!" he says.

Waters loved the job because he got to read all day and because Cook encouraged rudeness among her clerks. Cook and Norman Mailer were good friends, and Waters was told to be especially nasty to customers who dared to say anything bad about Mailer, whose books were popular at that time.

"I saw Molly snatch a book out of someone's hand and say, 'Get out!'" Waters recalls. "I was very impressed. I thought, *This is my kind of job!*"

When the skies were clear, Waters supplemented his income by shoplifting and by selling speed door-to-door on his bicycle. He'd met a local physician, Dr. Hiebert, who unwittingly supplied Waters with black beauties. "It wasn't that I was a major dealer," he says. "But back then, this was the only way to raise money for underground movies."

"He was very old and fell asleep examining people," Pearce says of Hiebert. "But speed was easily available. You could go into any doctor's mailbox and get free samples, or get it prescribed: It was either for depression or obesity, and everyone claimed to be fat or depressed."

Waters calls Hiebert "The notorious Dr. Feelgood of Provincetown," and says, "He was so old that he didn't remember how many times you came in to refill your prescription, and you could always give him a fake name for billing."

Waters ran into Sique Stole again, and Sique introduced him to her sister, Nancy, whom Waters would eventually rename Mink Stole. "She still looked normal at the time," Waters remembers. "But I could tell she was itching to break bad at any moment."

One of 10 kids, Nancy had recently attended Baltimore's all-girl Eastern High. She had graduated early but refused to attend the "boring" commencement ceremony. Now she was trying desperately to become a beatnik. She'd pierced her ears and wore Levi's—a daring fashion choice for a teenage girl at that time—and had just returned from a trip out west with a couple of druggie pals when she hitched a ride to Provincetown in a stolen Mustang.

"It was there that I met John Waters," she says, "proving what I've always said: You meet the best people on field trips."

Stole became engaged to 78-year-old Prescott Townsden, an eccentric gay liberationist who peddled homosexual propaganda from his motor scooter. The engagement didn't last—"There was speculation he might want children," Stole says—and she and Waters moved briefly to New York City, where they rented an apartment on Hudson Street. While she worked a day job, Waters worked his latest scam: He'd put on a pair of torn tennis shoes and head for local department stores, where he'd claim to have gotten his foot caught in their escalator.

Eventually, Waters ran out of department stores to dupe, and he and Stole returned to Baltimore. He moved back in with his parents, and found a job at a local Doubleday bookstore. And he began plotting his next picture.

Waters refers to *Roman Candles* as "my first real movie." The film is clearly influenced by Warhol's groundbreaking, triple-projected *Chelsea Girls,* and Waters himself has described the movie as "an obvious rip-off" of that picture. There's no story, just what the novice filmmaker called "home movies of my friends shoplifting, then modeling their shoplifted dresses—that kind of thing."

Those friends included Maelcum, Bonnie, and Mona, as well as several of Waters' newer chums: Mink, Pat Moran, David Lochary, Mark Isherwood, Bob Skidmore, and, in his movie debut, Divine. These would-be actors are showcased in random scenes: In one, Mink sobs at a graveside; in another, an obese woman named Alexis eats a bowl of fruit; Maelcum, dressed as a nun, drinks beer and makes out with a man dressed as a priest; Mona, in a bridal gown, simulates sex with Bob and Mark; and Pat dances to Nancy Sinatra's "These Boots Were Made for Walkin'" and spanks Mink, who's wearing a silver miniskirt. In other scenes, David reads *The Wizard of Oz* to Maelcum, who throws star fits, while Bob attacks Bonnie with an electric fan; a junkie is seen shooting heroin; and, finally, Maelcum plays hide-and-seek with Divine, who barely appears elsewhere in the film.

Waters shot much of *Roman Candles* in his bedroom, which he dubbed Dreamland Studios, on 8mm color and black-and-white film stolen by Mona. He added some stock footage—a Kuchar trademark—of the pope interspersed with bits of old horror movies, and constructed a soundtrack of old rock-and-roll songs, radio ads, and sound bites from a press conference with Lee Harvey Oswald's mother.

The 40-minute film is, in fact, three separate 8mm movies shown simultaneously on three screens. For archival purposes, Waters has recently had the film duped onto videotape, where it's split into four quadrants, with the fourth quadrant blank. But *Roman Candles* is not currently in circulation. In fact, it had only one three-show engagement, in 1966 at Baltimore's Flower Mart, an annual downtown celebration.

"The world premiere was much better than the movie," according to Waters, who convinced a forward-thinking reverend to screen *Roman Candles,* billed as "a trash epic," at the Episcopal Emmanuel Church. The movie sold out all three of its Flower Mart screenings, and was the subject of both a long feature and a review in *The Baltimore Sun.*

Invigorated, Waters and his gang, who were now calling themselves the Dreamlanders, began work on a spoof of *The Wizard of
Oz* (1939). Known alternately as *The Wizard of Odd* and *Dorothy,
the Kansas City Pothead,* the color film was quickly abandoned
after Waters realized the difficulties of synching a silent movie.
His plan to loop dialogue onto a reel-to-reel audio tape after the
silent film footage was shot proved too laborious and, although a
lengthy article about the making of the film appeared in *The
Baltimore Sun* (under the banner "The Wizard of Oz Goes to
Pot"), Waters dumped the project.

The surviving footage from *Dorothy* shows Pat Moran, in a
blue gingham dress, in the lead. Mink Stole plays Auntie Em,
Maelcum Sole is the Wicked Witch, and new Dreamlander
George Figgs plays the scarecrow.

After abandoning the project, Waters fled to Provincetown in
the summer of 1967, once again with Mona Montgomery in tow.
He took a job at the Provincetown Bookshop, where he was paid
$100 a week plus all the books he could read. "It was a great job,"
he says. "But the greatest thing was that every winter they closed
up, and I could go anywhere in the country and collect unem-
ployment, and some of the early movies were financed by that."

Waters' relationship with Montgomery was disintegrating, and
she returned to Baltimore halfway through the summer. He
moved in with Sique, who lived in a tree fort owned by Prescott
Townsden. The tree house had no roof or running water, and trees
grew up out of the living room floor. The fort was partly made
from an old submarine suspended in the branches of a large oak.
There were separate units, connected by gangplanks and reached
by a rope ladder. Waters lived in one "apartment" with Sique and
her friend Flo; Mink lived in another with Channing Wilroy, a
friend from Baltimore whom Waters had admired when Wilroy
was a regular on *The Buddy Deane Show,* Baltimore's version of
American Bandstand.

"We could all kick ourselves," Stole laments today. "There are no photographs of the tree fort. It burned down in 1969 or '70, and the town was so pleased that it was gone."

When Waters returned to Baltimore in the fall of 1967, he brought along Marina Melin, a sexy Swedish painter he'd befriended in Provincetown. The pair rented a slum apartment in downtown Baltimore, which they furnished with stolen antiques and dubbed the new Dreamland Studios. Waters bought a 16mm camera and began work on his next film, *Eat Your Makeup*.

"I got the idea from the Penny Patch, a candy store that I still go to when I'm in Provincetown," he says. "They sold candy lipstick with the little slogan, 'Eat Up Your Make Up.'"

Shot in 16mm black and white, the film stars Melin, Lochary, and Soul. *Eat Your Makeup* tells the story of a demented governess (Soul) and her boyfriend (Lochary) who kidnap models (Melin, Pearce, and Montgomery) and force them to model themselves to death in front of crowds of maniacs (Divine, among others). The models are given only makeup to eat, and they grovel shamelessly for a taste of eyeliner and cheap mascara.

In the film's most notorious scene, Waters recreates the John F. Kennedy assassination. The fantasy sequence—in which Divine portrays Jackie Kennedy—was inspired by the famous Zapruder film and predates Oliver Stone's similar homage in *JFK* by more than 20 years.

"We had the whole assassination scene, in which she climbs over the junk in the car, covered in blood," Waters told writer John Ives in 1992. "I have to get some magazine to dispute (Oliver Stone's) claim of being the first person to do the Kennedy assassination. He waited so long! We did it almost the next year!"

The film, filled with violence and antimedia messages, ends on a poignant note that foreshadows Waters' later fairy-tale imagery. After Melin, the last surviving model, dies on the runway, a cavalry officer places flowers on her body and kisses her. She awakens and, dressed as a fairy princess, strolls off into the woods.

Among Waters' favorite memories of *Eat Your Makeup* is the dope vending machine that he built for the film. "It was a machine that sold syringes," he says. "It actually says 'Dope' on each little vending window. My father helped me make it. Which is so odd, when I look back on it. My father is very Republican but very supportive. He actually helped me build this dope machine in 1967. I actually look back in awe that he did that."

Much of the film was shot on Waters' parents' front lawn— "'The Dreamland Lot,' as we called it"—and the sound was looped in Waters' ghetto apartment. On the first floor of the building was a plumbing school. "You had to walk right through it to get to the street," Waters says. "Plumbers would sit there working on pipes and we would walk through with, like, Divine in drag.

"We had to try to synchronize the sound on a tape to what they were saying on film, which was impossible. But I didn't know that then. The whole beginning of the movie is this girl just going 'makeup, makeup, oh, God, makeup…,' moaning about makeup for about three minutes. We had to try to synchronize that sequence to her lips moving, so we did it for like four or five days.

"The man in the plumbing store finally said to me, 'Well I heard that up there but I just thought it was one of your friends havin' a baby, so I didn't say anything.'"

During the film's crude postproduction, Marina Melin suffered a nervous breakdown and was hospitalized. Although drug abuse was cited as the reason for her poor health, Waters believes that the monotony of the sound dubbing process contributed greatly to Melin's collapse.

"Finally, Marina said to me, 'John, I've actually eaten my makeup.' I knew something was wrong when she started wearing evening gowns and tiaras just to go downstairs to empty the garbage in the morning."

When Waters entered *Eat Your Makeup* in a student film competition, the judges went berserk. They shut down the movie before it ended and tried to prevent the film from being shown at

its local church premiere the following week. When church officials refused to cancel the screening, the judges, acting as a self-
appointed film censor board, telephoned the Internal Revenue
Service. Citing the church's nonprofit status, IRS agents refused
to allow Waters to charge admission. A hat was passed after each
of the film's three screenings, but audiences were so offended by
the Kennedy sequence that few were generous.

Jacqueline Kennedy may have been aware of the film: When
Divine attended a party in Jackie's honor some 16 years later, she
blatantly refused to speak to Divine. Furious at the snub, Divine
told *People* magazine that Jackie had glared at him all evening
"because we were wearing the same dress."

Waters took the only existing print of *Eat Your Makeup* with
him to Provincetown that summer, and most of the Dreamlanders
followed. He rented a small cottage with Pearce on Mechanic
Street and returned to his job at the Provincetown Bookshop.
When he arranged a screening of *Eat Your Makeup* at a local
church, the bookshop's owners let him turn the entire front window of the store into a giant ad for the film.

To promote the screening, Waters and Bonnie walked up and
down Commercial Street, handing out fliers for the movie along
with little candy lipsticks. "I went in and bought out every candy
lipstick," Waters says. "I would hand people a flier, she would
hand them a candy lipstick, and say, 'Eat it, read it, and come.'"

Although some refused the candy—"People thought we were
giving them drugs!" Waters recalls—the Provincetown showing
was sold out. Despite the film's warm P-town reception, Waters
knew it would never be a hit. "It was too fucked-up and arty," he
says, an opinion shared by the manager of New York's Gate
Theater when, in hopes of a booking, Waters screened it for her.

The 45-minute featurette is impossible to screen, because the
finished film is shot at sixteen frames per second and the synchronized sound is recorded on a separate tape. Waters says he
doesn't want to see *Eat Your Makeup* released commercially,

although he admits he sometimes runs the film for close friends who come to visit.

"It's fun to show," he told journalist Jack Stevenson in 1988. "It's like showing home movies to your old friends. In my apartment, to people I've known for 20 years, it's fun to watch. To put it in a theater or in front of an audience, I'm sure that there'd be a few people that would enjoy it. But basically it's much better to imagine it."

Back in Baltimore, the pleasure of another successful opening was quickly forgotten when Maelcum Soul abruptly died. In *Shock Value,* Waters claims that Soul died "of old age," even though she was only 28 at the time of her death.

Soul had been Waters' first star, and her influence was felt in Waters' next several films—particularly in the look and attitude of his new leading lady, who happened to be a man. Waters had noticed that audiences for *Eat Your Makeup* had reacted favorably to Glenn's small role in the film, and had made a mental note: *Give Divine more screen time.*

"I responded to what people liked," Waters says. "I knew from *Eat Your Makeup* that people started to recognize Divine. From then on, I just always had him in the lead. He was my new star."

Chapter Four
DIVINING DIVINE

"I CAN NEVER REPLACE DIVINE. THERE'S NO PERSON ON EARTH LIKE HIM."

—John Waters

The woman who answers the door is wearing a tube top and a denim skirt. She has crayon-red lips, hair scrunchies around each wrist, and huge dark circles under her eyes. She's wedged a cordless telephone between her tattooed shoulder and her ear, and she's shouting into it as she waves me into the room.

Inside, Calvin Sharpee's waiting area is crowded with plastic palm trees. The walls are covered with paint-by-number art: framed landscapes, cute clowns, and a pair of pixies alongside mottled portraits of George and Martha Washington. I sit facing a colossal, fluorescent Last Supper and wait for someone to tell me what to do.

I've come here to speak with Divine, who has been dead for 12 years.

Calvin Sharpee is a spiritual medium who specializes in channeling deceased celebrities, among them Divine, whom I've been trying to contact for several weeks. I've traveled thousands of miles to see Calvin, who got my name and number from one of his colleagues—the only one of them who didn't laugh at me or hang up when I called to ask if they could put me in touch with a famous dead drag queen.

Calvin sent me his media kit—a blurrily photocopied list of dead celebrities with whom he is on speaking terms—and a photograph of himself in a turban. Divine does not appear on Calvin's list of "Stars Now Appearing in the Beyond," but I notice that Larry Storch, who is still very much alive, does. I decide not to mention this when I call to make my appointment.

Calvin has agreed to let me speak with Divine, but on certain conditions: I'm to come alone, pay cash up front, and I must refrain from using the words "heaven" and "hell" during my interview. I'm also forbidden to use Calvin's real name if I write about my visit. He doesn't want to become known, he tells me, as a medium who specializes in "transgendered" spirits.

"I have no trouble with homosexuals," Calvin lisps, when he joins me in the cramped waiting area several minutes later. "I just don't want them lining up outside to talk to late, lamented drag queens from some neighborhood bar. I do *celebrities*. Every one of my clients was listed with SAG or AFTRA when they were here on earth."

Calvin settles onto a small, faux leopard settee. He's built like a linebacker: 6 foot 2 and 250 pounds, all of them poured into a paisley caftan that's tied shut with a tasseled bell cord. His only small features are his mouth, which appears to be lipsticked, and his dainty hands, which sport a ring on every finger.

He explains that he'll begin by contacting his familiar, Betty, who acts as a sort of otherworldly middleman in all his transactions. Betty will then put us through to Divine, whom Calvin says has agreed to speak with me for "up to 30 minutes." Calvin shows me into a converted bedroom, and as we take our seats at a low table, I ask if Divine is getting a cut of the $500 I've paid to interview him.

Calvin narrows his eyes and quickly stands. "If you're going to make jokes," he spits, hands on hips, "I must ask you to leave. This is very serious business, and not some scene from a John Waters movie. I'll thank you to keep your asides to yourself."

I grovel and curtsy, and eventually Calvin returns to his seat. "It's just that it's important to maintain the proper mood while speaking with the beyond," he sighs, smoothing his caftan. "Most people come here on a lark. Last week we had a bachelor party, a bunch of drunks who stopped here on their way to a dubious nightclub because the bridegroom wanted to sleep with Natalie Wood before he got married. It's just too much. I'm a professional who deserves a certain amount of respect, not some cheap sideshow people can come here and laugh at."

I assure Calvin that I didn't mean any harm, that I was just trying to lighten the mood. Maybe, I suggest, I was a little nervous about meeting a famous dead person.

Calvin shudders. "Please don't use that word here," he says. "We prefer to think of the spirits we contact as people who have simply relocated. They used to live in Beverly Hills, and now they live in the beyond."

I start to ask how I'll know when I'm talking to Divine—"Will Calvin's voice change pitch? Will he suddenly apply even more eyeliner than he's already wearing?"—but he shushes me. "It's time to contact Betty," he says, then abruptly slumps over, his forehead smacking the tabletop with a bang.

After a while, Calvin lifts his head and, with his eyes wide open, holds a conversation with himself in two different voices. Betty, in a nasal twang, complains about the chair Calvin's sitting in and asks after his cat; Calvin tells Betty that the cat is pregnant again and promises to sit on a throw pillow the next time he contacts her. Finally, he mentions "our appointment," and Betty gets down to business.

"Yes, yes, Divine's right here beside me," Calvin says in Betty's voice. "But he wants you to tell the nice reporter please not to ask him about...oh, dear, I don't quite know how to say this."

Calvin shifts quickly into another, instantly recognizable voice: a dead-on impersonation of Divine, which seems to come from way in back of Calvin's throat.

"Go on, Hon. You can say it," Calvin-as-Divine says. "Tell him I don't want no questions about eating dog shit!"

I promise Divine I won't mention poop of any kind.

Calvin smiles, settles back in his chair, and purrs, "OK, Mr. Reporter. Turn on that tape recorder and ask me some questions!"

What can you tell me about where you live now?

Well, the weather's nice. And there's lots of good restaurants. But there's not much to do here. There's bowling, and singing lessons. Oh, and Wednesday is Holy Torment Day.

Holy Torment Day?

You know, you get to torture and maim anyone who was really mean to you while you were still alive. I'm working my way through all the boys who beat me up in junior high. I'm practicing up for Cher's arrival!

So you're happy?

Well, it's not what I thought it would be. I figured it would be all swimming pools, limousines, and servants. But everyone's so liberal here. There's no working class, so it's fend for yourself! I sure wish one of my really big fans would get hit by a bus so I could get some help up here.

Do you get recognized there?

Yes, and by all the worst people too. I'm dead, I shouldn't have to talk to Arthur Treacher, you know what I'm saying? So I mostly stay in and watch TV. Like I said, there isn't a whole lot to do after your three wishes. I mean, there's really no organized activity.

Three wishes?

Uh-huh. They grant you three wishes when you first get up here.

Who does?

Well, the people who grant the wishes, that's who!

OK.

So I wish I had used my wishes for different things. More *lasting* things. But I thought, *Well, I can just wish for more wishes, so what the hell,* right?

What did you wish for?

My first wish was for a big fat cream pie. I was starving! I ate the whole thing right there. Then I wished for a crown, with real rubies and diamonds and a great big lapis right in the center. I wanted to be the queen of heaven! I started to think about ice cream and soda and fruit-frosted cupcakes, and I shouted, "Third wish! More wishes!" and a big buzzer went off and some big guy with fake-looking wings snatched off my crown and that was that, I was off to be fitted for my tunic and handed my harp. No one told me you could get busted for the seven deadly sins. Disqualified for being greedy!

That's too bad.

You're telling me. It ain't fair. Joan Crawford asked for a movie house. She got one, but she only shows her own movies there. Sounds like vanity to me! I used to go to her theater a lot, but I haven't been in a while. I mean, how many times can you sit through *Ice Follies of 1939*?

So you've met Joan Crawford?

She works the candy counter! She looks pretty good too. Joan sure was smart with them other two wishes. Her second wish was for a mirror. And when she saw what she looked like—because, you know, they don't bother to tell you that up here you look pretty much like you did the day you died. Anyway, I guess Joan looked sort of like an apple doll when she arrived. Kind of dried up. So she got her mirror, and she screamed—I heard you could hear her all the way to Borneo—and then her next wish was that she was 27 again. Let me tell you, you haven't lived until you've bought Junior Mints from Mildred Pierce.

Do you see any of the other Dreamlanders there?

I had lunch with David Lochary a couple of times. He's very popular here. He does all the stars' hair—Vera Hruba Ralston and Inger Stevens and Ellen Corby. He told me his secret fantasy: He can't wait for Olivia de Havilland and Joan Fontaine to die. He's going to book them at the same time in his salon, in facing chairs. But I told him, "David, honey, you just forget that plan. That De Havilland bitch will never make it up here."

What about Edie? Is she up there?

I don't know. She might be. We were never all that close, so it's not like she'd look me up. I mean, when I first got here, I sort of expected she'd call or something, welcome me to the neighborhood. Maybe she's…*elsewhere.*

Do you work?

Well, no one makes movies up here, if that's what you mean. It's all cabaret acts and showcases. For a while there, Totie Fields and

I were talking about a revival of *Three Girls Three* with Cornelia Otis Skinner, but Totie lost interest. I'd love to be in John Waters' next picture, but he never calls.

But you're...

I know, I'm dead. You think Mae West was alive when she made *Sextette*? I just need a good agent.

Are you still fat?

I don't have *size*. I am everything, and I am nothing. I am the air and the trees and the shit under your shoes. And I'll tell you a secret: Just because you're a sycamore doesn't mean you don't still crave Moon Pies.

What's the best thing about being dead?

Well, you don't have to work some crummy job. Down there, I was a prisoner to a sequin tube dress. Up here no one wants to hear me yell over a disco track. I mostly bask. Plus I have a lot of social engagements. Today I'm lunching with Dagmar and Oscar Homolka. Tomorrow it's dinner with Helen Twelvetrees.

What do you miss?

Well, it's hard to find good makeup here. Shoes are no problem; Jeff Chandler runs a store that's all ladies things in men's sizes. That's nice. But everything's a variation on white up here, and the clerks just laugh if you shoplift. So what's the point?

What was the biggest disappointment in your life?

Look, I'm not suffering from a head cold. I'm *dead*. You want to talk about disappointing?

So, did you, uh, fulfill your destiny while you were here on earth?

Well, I got to be famous, and I got to wear a lot of wigs. That part was good. And the drugs were fun; we don't have those here, of course. The Catholic Church won't allow it. I guess I had a pretty good time. But I left there with a lot of unanswered questions.

Like?

Well, what does *chili size* mean? You see that on menus: *chili size*. But what does it mean? And who came up with the name Fingerhut? My mother used to get Fingerhut catalogs in the mail. It sounds like a place where you'd get your nails done.

Who do you miss?

No one. My dogs. I don't know. Next question!

So there are no pets there?

Well, sure there are. But you sort of get *assigned* your pets up here. You don't, you know, get to...I mean, there's no little pet store here, where you can go and pick out a little puppy.

So you were assigned some pets?

Uh-huh. I have a sea horse and a vole.

A vole?

It's like a groundhog. Anyway, yes, we have pets here. My vole is named Natasha, and she likes Dolly Madison snack cakes best. I haven't named the sea horse yet, but I have nothing but time, Hon.

I guess so. So does being dead give you a new perspective on life?

Well, here's something I discovered after I died: All your worst fears about the government are true. They *do* run everything, and it *is* all a conspiracy. The government is run by evil assholes who do mean stuff just because they're in a bad mood. They're murderers. Murderers and rapists! People who are entirely above the law because they...because they know they can get away with it! The government killed JonBenet! Some president's aide had a niece who was competing against the kid in some Little Miss Dingleball pageant, and bam! The next thing you know, JonBenet is six feet under. The government is hiding an entire alien race under a shopping mall in Duluth. And the government is behind *Entertainment Tonight* too! Have you noticed the anchors all look alike? John Tesh left the show, here comes another guy who looks just like him. It's a conspiracy, I tell you!

How do you know this?

Well, when I was still there, on earth, they told me. But I didn't believe them.

They told you?

Yes. They came to me in the night, because I was a fat drag queen who threw mackerel and ate dog shit in films. And they would come to me in the night, secret agents, people from Washington dressed in cheap suits. They would lean in my window while I slept and they would whisper to me, "Listen, fatty. You either stop with the movies or we'll stop *you*."

You must have been frightened by this?

Well, it did give one pause. One time, during my nightclub act, a big black guy got up onstage while I was singing. And he grabbed me and kissed me, and while he was kissing me he yelled into my ear, "The president wants you dead, fat bitch! He hates high heels, and he hates disco, and you're our next target!" I could barely go on! I left the stage and there was the most beautiful Puerto Rican boy waiting for me there. I thought, *Is this my killer?* But it turned out he was there for an entirely different reason, if you know what I mean.

Which president was that? Bush?

Oh, who remembers? But the restaurant me and the Puerto Rican boy went to after we became better acquainted was yummy.

If they make a motion picture of your life story, who would you like to see play you?

George Clooney.

How would things be different if you were still alive?

I would have taken over the entire entertainment industry by now. Elizabeth Taylor would be my servant. Richard Simmons would have been brutally murdered by my personal assistant. And George Figgs would be president!

Do you have any regrets?

[*Mumbles*] That fur coat. The fur coat. I regret that.

That you never had one?

[*Silence*]

That you left one behind somewhere?

[*No response*]

Do you mean Mink Stole?

No! Not *her*. [*Long pause*] It was a coat I gave my mother. Just before I came here. And I don't want to talk about it.

I'm sorry. It's just—

I said I don't wanna talk about it.

I'm sorry. I was just trying to—

You know…I'm not so sure about you. I dunno if I wanna *do* this interview. You're being awfully nosy. Does John Waters know you're writin' a book about him? I might just have to call him up about you. We got phones here, you know. *Big* phones.

Phones in heaven?

I wish you wouldn't call it that.

What?

Heaven.

What should I call it then?

Dreamland, honey. I'm in Dreamland.

Just then, Calvin's nose begins to run. A runner of snot flows from his left nostril as Betty's matronly voice crackles through. "I'm sorry, dear. It appears that Divine has...gone. He seemed pretty upset. Star fits, you know."

Calvin dabs daintily at his nose with a Kleenex. "Dang cold," Betty says. "Well, I think I'll go now, Calvin, if you're through with me. There's some guy in Cleveland who wants to talk to Freddie Prinze, and I'd like to get a load of wash in before he calls."

Calvin slumps forward again. I switch off my portable tape recorder and wait for him to come to. But he never awakens. After about 10 minutes, I stand and head for the door. I figure I'll let the guy sleep; being three people at once must be exhausting.

As I pass the reception desk, I notice that the woman who let me in is also asleep, her head resting on her gaudily manicured hands. Just before I reach her, she straightens up, looks me straight in the eye and says, in Calvin's voice, "I *told* you not to mention heaven!"

Chapter Five
SOME SORT OF DISCOVERY

"During the late '60s, I felt like a fish out of water."
—John Waters

"Every once in a while I'm tempted to take it out of distribution," John Waters has said of *Mondo Trasho,* his first feature film. "But what the hell, it's already out there. And there are parts of it I like."

Filmed in 1969, *Mondo Trasho* is told almost entirely in visuals, with occasional sound cues and a "wild track" of rock music and bits of dialogue. Waters claims he'd like the movie better if it were shorter. "It's 90 minutes long, and it should have been 20. It's got 20 minutes of good footage in it. It takes Mary Vivian Pearce an *hour* to get to the bus."

But *Mondo Trasho's* real-time exploits are part of the movie's charm. It's Waters' most unpolished, naïve work, and arguably his artiest film. Some critics have questioned the movie's "complicated" plot, but in fact *Mondo Trasho* barely has a plot at all. The 93-minute film tells the story of a young woman (Pearce) who—like so many of Water's heroines—is having a lousy day. She has a pleasant sexual experience with a stranger in the park, then is run over by a woman (Divine, driving a 1959 Cadillac convertible) who spends the rest of the afternoon trying to get help for herself and her victim. In a series of stunning visuals, the pair encounter a mad doctor, a topless dancer, reporters from *The National Enquirer,* and the Virgin Mother of God. They visit a Laundromat, an insane asylum, and a pigpen. One of them ends up dead, the other disfigured.

Divine, younger and thinner than he ever appeared again, is delightful as the buxom innocent whose day is wrecked by fate. And Mink Stole, in her brief bits here, is captivating. Her topless tap dance routine is the film's high point, and perhaps the only moment when we're tempted to tear our eyes away from Divine.

The movie's meager press materials from 1969 (authored by Waters himself) call it a "combination of cheap theatrics, obsessional fantasies, and a true love of all that is trashy in film today." More than 30 years after *Mondo Trasho*'s brief theatrical release, Waters is less enthusiastic about his first full-length film. He grudgingly admits, "If you've seen all my other films, I guess it's OK to see that one. The very first time we showed it, people didn't especially like it."

Today, Waters fans love the film, which signaled the beginning of his real work with Divine. Although he'd appeared in Waters' earlier short films, the former Glenn Milstead truly became a star in this one. (Upon the film's release, a critic at *The Los Angeles Free Press* wrote, "The 300 pound sex symbol, Divine, is undoubtedly some sort of discovery.")

In order to concentrate on his first lead role, Divine quit his job as a hairdresser and moved back in with his parents. He told them that his doctor had ordered him to stop styling hair because it "made him nervous," and the Milsteads welcomed Glenn back home. Waters borrowed the film's $2,000 budget from his father and, for the first time ever, *purchased* rather than shoplifted the film he used to shoot his movie. He also bought a pair of gold, six-inch spike heels from Frederick's of Hollywood for Divine to wear in several scenes.

Stole, set to play one of the asylum inmates in the picture, hand-copied Waters' handwritten scripts, which he distributed to his cast. Waters asked Pearce to play the unfortunate beauty who spends most of the film unconscious. David Lochary created the role of crazy Dr. Coat Hanger, and Waters' boyfriend, John Leisenring, agreed to appear as the pervert who accosts Pearce in the park. With Divine in the lead and several of Waters' other friends rounding out the cast, the young director began shooting in the winter of 1968.

Waters regrets the movie's opening scene, in which an ax-wielding man in executioner's garb slaughters chickens. "That's the most hideous thing I've ever filmed," he says. "It's something I'm a little ashamed of, because it's really cruel. I understand people being upset about that."

Although many consider the film's windup, in which Pearce is left with monster feet that have been grafted on by a mad doctor, to be unnecessarily gloomy, Waters disagrees. "She gets *magic* feet, you see. And those magic feet bring her happiness and take her to all different places. But the best thing in *Mondo Trasho* is Divine crawling through pig shit at the end, when the Virgin Mary appears. Actually, it was so erotic that the pigs started to fuck each other while we were filming. You can see that in the shot. I couldn't believe it turned them on. It was like porno for pigs."

"This was the movie that convinced my mother I had dedicated my life to ruining hers," Stole remembers wryly. "She didn't see it, but one of my older sisters did and ratted on me."

Waters refers to *Mondo Trasho* as his "gutter film," because so much of it was shot in alleyways and on deserted Baltimore streets. Stole remembers, "John shot a lot of scenes in Laundromats in those days, because the lighting there was good." That Waters was paying attention to such details as lighting can be attributed to Pete Garey, owner of Baltimore's Quality Film Labs Inc., whom Waters had approached about learning the basic techniques of filmmaking.

"Pete Garey was my film school," Waters says today. "Here was someone who made me sign papers that said he wasn't responsible for the footage I shot, in case we were arrested. He had signs in his shop window during the Vietnam war that read 'Bomb Hanoi.' He was hardly sympathetic to the kind of movies I was making, but incredibly sympathetic and patient in trying to teach me how to do it. Nobody else told me how to do *anything*."

During filming, much of the cast was arrested. Early in the shoot, Waters staged a scene in which Divine imagines that a roadside hitchhiker is naked. "Back then, the only way to put a nude hitchhiker on the screen was to actually film one," Stole says. "So we set up that scene on the campus of Johns Hopkins University, without permission, of course."

As Waters filmed Dreamlander Mark Isherwood, who played the hitchhiker, standing naked by the side of the road, the campus police arrived. "A couple of grad students took offense when they saw us and called security," Stole says. "We managed to elude the campus cops, but a '59 Eldorado is hard to hide, and we were picked up when we tried to return the borrowed car to its owner."

Only Isherwood was taken to jail, but Waters, Stole, and Lochary were arrested the following day. The official charge filed by the Baltimore police was "conspiracy to commit indecent exposure," and the American Civil Liberties Union picked up the case. In a crafty move meant to prove that Waters was not a pornographer, ACLU representatives demanded that the district attorney watch *Hag in a Black Leather Jacket,* which Waters dutifully screened for the courtroom. The trick worked.

"The DA's staff realized I was just a crackpot with a camera," Waters later reported. "And they wanted to save face by getting out of the whole mess with a minimum of bad press."

Judge Solomon Bliss dismissed the case by reciting to the stunned crowd a poem he'd written that read, in part:

Old Baltimore is in a spin
Because of Isherwood's display of skin
He cannot bear the shame and cracks
Brought on by showing the bare facts.

The incident, an invaluable (if unplanned) publicity stunt, was widely reported. Locally, *The Baltimore Sun* covered the incident. Lochary reportedly told his jailer, "Your stage is great, but can't you do something about these dressing rooms?" The national press, including *Playboy, Variety* (in a story headlined "Balto *Mondo Trasho* in Campus Pincho of Its Figleafed Hero"), and *The News American* quickly picked up the story.

The film's notoriety led to a sellout premiere, once again staged at Baltimore's Emmanuel Church in early 1969. *Mondo Trasho*'s good notices caught the attention of the New York–based Film-Makers Cooperative, which booked the film for a brief midnight screening in Los Angeles. For the first time, Waters' work was being seen outside of Baltimore and Provincetown, a fact that wasn't lost on *New Yorker* film critic Pauline Kael. She saw the picture and was among the first nationally published critics to acknowledge Waters' peculiar genius. Although Kael didn't review the movie, she gave it—and Waters' fledgling career—a shot in the arm later that year when she referred to Federico Fellini's *Satyricon* as "Fellini's *Mondo Trasho*."

Waters took his new movie with him to Provincetown that summer, where he convinced the manager of the Art Cinema to book *Mondo Trasho* as a midnight movie. Meanwhile, the Film-Makers Cooperative had arranged for the film to play Boston's Kenmore Square, so Waters had to drag the film's only existing print back and forth between screenings, accompanied by various Dreamlanders, who handed out fliers promoting the film.

"When it was in the Art theater, I had to guarantee my percentage of every seat," Waters says. "If nobody came, I'd owe thousands of dollars. But we sold out every time. The owner was sort of astonished. But the cast and I really went out and worked to sell it."

Promoting the early films was hard work that would later become something of a tradition. The Dreamlanders would dress up in wild costumes and pass out fliers before every screening, while Waters once again turned the window of the Provincetown Bookshop into a giant billboard.

Pat Moran recalls that the group did "wild posting," which found them sneaking around at night and tacking up posters all over town and slipping fliers onto car windshields. "Or we'd do what we called 'the plate job,' where we'd go to a college cafeteria and bombard unsuspecting students with fliers. We did these sort of promotions right up through *Cry-Baby*."

Door prizes were another favorite gimmick at Waters' premieres, with the winner usually gifted with a free meal for two at a local greasy spoon. "We'd give away dinners to the worst restaurant in town," he says, "like the Doggie Diner in San Francisco. People loved it."

The winner of the door prize—dinner for two at the seedy Little Tavern—at *Mondo Trasho*'s Baltimore premiere was Dorothy Karen Mueller, a mean hippie whose friends called her Cookie. Waters and Cookie, who had just been released from a mental hospital, became fast friends, and Cookie became a Dreamlander.

"John and I once shared a lover," Cookie told a reporter several years later. "That's how I got to know him really well. John was in love with this guy and I was in love with the same guy. We were very jealous of each other and that's how I really got to know him."

When they weren't promoting their new movies that summer, the Dreamlanders were up to no good. While Mink Stole ran credit card scams, David Lochary faked falls in restaurants and demanded insurance money. Waters bought traveler's checks, reported them stolen, and doubled his income. Mary Vivian Pearce stole bicycles.

"I almost got caught selling a stolen bike," Pearce says. "The police took me in and questioned me. Somehow they believed me when I told them I'd bought it from a dishwasher."

Aside from the occasional bust, the summer of 1969 was uneventful for the Dreamlanders. "We shoplifted and took speed," Pearce says. "And we all got crabs that summer. There was John, boiling his underwear! And John and I got scabies too.

The doctor told John he hadn't seen a case since migrant workers in the 1930s."

Once rid of their various vermin, the Dreamlanders returned to Baltimore. Waters paid back the $2,000 he'd borrowed from his father, bought a new sound camera, and began work on his first "talkie."

Having already documented JFK's assassination, Waters was anxious to revisit true crime and celebrity death in his next movie. Although he rarely discusses *The Diane Linkletter Story* (and in fact doesn't mention the film at all in *Shock Value*), his first talkie represents a pivotal point in Waters' career. The movie was shot on October 5, 1969, the day after Diane Linkletter, the 20-year-old daughter of television host Art Linkletter, fell to her death from a skyscraper.

In interviews, Pearce has referred to *The Diane Linkletter Story* as a "sound rehearsal," an experimental film shot to test Waters' new synchronized sound equipment. Waters says he was inspired to make the film because of "the obvious news event and the fact that I was testing a camera the day after she jumped."

There was no script. The dialogue, such as it is, was improvised by the actors: Lochary as Art Linkletter, Pearce as his wife, Lois, and Divine—in ridiculous hippie rags and a crooked wig—in the title role. In the 17-minute movie, Art and Lois are seated in their tacky home (actually Waters' latest Baltimore apartment), muttering and exclaiming about their young daughter, who's been out partying all night with "that fast crowd." When she arrives home, Diane is wrecked on acid—"I'm on LSD!"—and waxing poetic about her new boyfriend, who has a groovy car. Art, incensed, calls the police, and Lois slaps her. Diane runs upstairs to her room and leaps from her second-story window.

Waters' version of Diane Linkletter's death is almost entirely fiction. While it's true that she jumped out of a window while on LSD, she wasn't at her parents' home at the time. She leapt from the kitchen window of her sixth-floor Shoreham Towers apartment in West Hollywood. And the suicide wasn't provoked by an argument with her parents. Alone in her apartment and tripping on acid, she decided her "brain was being destroyed" and telephoned her brother, Robert. She described her intention to commit suicide, screamed, and jumped out the window. Diane's boyfriend, Edward Durston ("Jim" in Waters' movie), arrived at the apartment just as she was preparing to jump. He grabbed the belt loop of her dress, but it ripped and she fell to her death.

While *The Diane Linkletter Story* is historically important, it's not much fun to watch. Pearce and Lochary spend most of the first 10 minutes of the film ad-libbing tediously—it was, after all, a sound rehearsal. The film picks up only when Divine enters, wearing shades and a serious 5 o'clock shadow.

On the other hand, the film's opening credits are hilarious. As Divine mugs shamelessly, the soundtrack plays awkwardly edited excerpts from "Dear Mom and Dad," an unbelievably tacky spoken-word record by the real-life Art and Diane Linkletter. Divine snorts cocaine, smokes hashish, and flashes peace signs while posting the film's handwritten titles, as Art and Diane speak in sincere tones: "Since being away, I've met a lot of weirdos—pot smokers and speed freaks. But I've found out how to tell the beautiful people from the phonies!" All the while, sappy music plays in the background.

The Diane Linkletter Story received what Waters calls "a couple of very underground screenings" and then was quickly shelved. The film has resurfaced in recent years as a bootleg video, usually coupled with Divine's stage play *The Neon Woman*. Although Waters dismisses the film, it's the first in his oeuvre to employ a theme he'd revisit throughout his career: a standoff between good and evil, in this case typified by the generation gap. Freethinking teen Diane is pitted against her uptight parents, who—like Penny Pingleton's in *Hairspray* and Wanda Wood's in *Cry-Baby*—attempt to curb their daughter's wild ways.

Pleased with the sync-sound of *Diane Linkletter* and confi-
dent with his new camera equipment, Waters borrowed another
$5,000 from his father and turned his attention to his first fea-
ture-length sound film. This time his inspiration came from the
burgeoning hippie culture, which Waters despised. While he
was tuned in to the political issues of his generation, he was
appalled by the lethargic conformity of the peacenik and hippie
movements.

"It was such a different time," John Waters says of the period, which saw the rise of porno chic—with films like *I Am
Curious (Yellow)* (1967) and *Deep Throat* (1972)—and the political victory of Richard Nixon. "There was a kind of cultural war
going on. It was the Yippie years of politics, with all those
actions against the government by people like Abbie Hoffman.
And all this Yippie radicalism was done with theatrics, which
certainly influenced me regarding style as terrorism. Everything
was peace and love. Whatever you did, you didn't commit violence. Those people always got on my nerves, even though I
wasn't violent, ever."

Although he'd started out liking the beatnik movement ("I was
into the whole Abbie Hoffman thing, completely. I would go to
Yale and set fires just for the fun of it"), Waters was now as
offended by the restrictions of hippie society as he was with the
mainstream culture he disdained. Ironically, his audience at the
time was mostly made up of counterculture dropouts who were
attracted to Waters' outsider vision. He provided this crowd with
an outlet for their anger by allowing them to laugh at the pro-
establishment nonsense prevalent then. At the same time, he
sneered at these would-be revolutionaries and their antiwar
marches and tedious be-ins, and depicted them in his films as
brainwashed losers.

When actress Sharon Tate was brutally murdered in Los
Angeles, Waters decided to work the murders into his new
movie, which he was calling *Multiple Maniacs*. He decided to

attribute the as yet unsolved murders to Divine in the picture.

"I figured that if the murderers were never caught, there would always be the possibility that maybe Divine really did do it," Waters says. "I wanted to scare the world."

The film's title, inspired by the Herschell Gordon Lewis' slasher pic *2,000 Maniacs,* refers to a band of vengeful lunatics, several of whom take the names of the actors portraying them. Billed as the Cavalcade of Perversion and led by a black-wigged Divine, the group—a degenerate circus with acts like the Puke Eater and the Armpit Licker—travels the country robbing and murdering its audiences. Divine has convinced her bitchy boyfriend, Mr. David (Lochary), who is having an affair with a woman named Bonnie (Pearce), that he helped her kill Sharon Tate. The usual Watersian mayhem quickly erupts: A series of rapes and murders is punctuated by an atrocious sex act in a church, the appearance of a huge boiled lobster, and a lot of hilarious dialogue. In the final shot—inspired by *Godzilla* and other cheesy giant-monster movies—a berserk Divine is gunned down by the National Guard.

"We were trying to do what the Manson family did, only with a movie camera," Waters says of *Multiple Maniacs.* "We wanted to scare the world. And you can see that rage, which was very antihippie."

One can also see the influence of Vincent Peranio, a new friend of Waters who would act as art director on all his subsequent films. An art school dropout, Peranio was hired to build Lobstora, the giant boiled lobster that rapes Divine in the film's final sequence. Peranio and his brother Ed animated Lobstora by both climbing inside the giant crayfish; their feet are visible in several shots of the finished film.

"There was a postcard that I always used to see on Cape Cod that showed a beach with a giant lobster dinner superimposed in the sky above it," Waters says. "That's where I got the idea for Lobstora."

Peranio introduced Waters to Susan Lowe, a slutty artist's model, and Edith Massey, an elderly barmaid at Pete's Hotel in downtown Baltimore. Waters was so taken with Edith that he cast her in a small role in *Multiple Maniacs*; like most of the rest of the cast, she essentially plays herself in the film.

Massey, a former B-girl, was raised in an orphanage and later did time in reform school. Among her many colorful careers was a stint as a madam in a sleazy Chicago whorehouse. After *Multiple Maniacs*, she quit bartending and opened a thrift store, Edith's Shopping Bag, in downtown Baltimore.

More than a little addle-brained, Massey had trouble memorizing her lines. She solved the problem by writing her dialogue over and over again in longhand. Waters recalls that Massey would occasionally blow a scene by reading the script direction as well as her dialogue.

Waters, still a puppeteer at heart, drove his players relentlessly during filming. He chastised any actor who forgot his lines, but always apologized later for losing his temper. He staged full rehearsals, as if he were directing a stage play, and demanded that his actors repeat their lines over and over until they were spoken exactly as Waters had intended them.

"He was very strict," Pearce recalls. "He acted out all the parts for each of us. And he was a good actor. Better than any of us."

Divine, as usual, was a trooper. During a long shoot in a church pew—throughout which he was bent over double, with no lines other than repeated orgasmic hoots—he never complained. Nor did he protest when asked to chew on a cow heart (supposedly the heart of Mr. David, whom Divine has murdered) which, having been left unrefrigerated, had spoiled.

The scene with Divine bent over double in the church, of course, is the infamous scene in which Mink Stole, playing a "religious whore," performs a "rosary job" on Divine. Prior to that scene, having just been raped by a pair of lunatics from the Cavalcade, Divine meets the Infant of Prague, who escorts her to the safety of a nearby church, where she undergoes a religious conversion. Mink, who is lurking in a nearby confessional, sidles up to Divine and, as Divine explains in the soundtrack, "inserts her rosary into one of my most private parts."

Stole had trouble hitting her mark during the scene. "I didn't have contact lenses, and didn't want to wear glasses, so I was blind as a bat on camera. I knew Divine was sitting a certain number of pews up from where I started, and the only way to hit my mark was to count one, two, three, until I got to the right pew. Then I slid in and said my lines."

Stole recalls Waters' attention to detail in the scene's final moments, which find her wiping off the rosary on a lace hankie. "For the last take of the scene, John, never one to miss an opportunity, pulled out a fudge candy bar to smear on the rosary."

Waters would continue to spoof religion in his films, but never again in such a vulgar way. "I'd like to think that got it out of my system," he's said of the rosary job. "Because there is no scene more blasphemous than that in any movie you can show me. And it still is really rude."

Waters is less proud of the final shot in the sequence, which depicts a man shooting up on the church altar as Divine and Mink exit. "It was the most gratuitous shot in any of my movies," he says. "It's there for no reason, just one more horrible thing."

Among those who found the entire film a "horrible thing" upon its release was Mary Avara, secretary of the Maryland State Board of Censors. "Oh, my God! That was really disgraceful!" she hollers, 30 years later. "I was sick over that. Sex in a church, my God, how low can you get?" Avara's case against the film was so persuasive that *Multiple Maniacs* was banned in Baltimore until 1981, when a local judge decided it could be shown at midnight at the Charles Theater.

"I used to fight with the censor board all the time," Waters recalls. "Mary Avara would say, 'You have to cut that vagina!' and

I'd say, 'That's a man. It's not a vagina, it's a cheater.' I'd have to explain that a cheater was a fake pubic thing that goes over a penis with a merkin on top, which was a pubic hair wig, which I'd try to explain to her just to horrify her. She'd scream, 'Don't tell me about sex, I was married to an Italian!' I'd spend every penny I had to make a movie and she'd hand me a pair of scissors and make me ruin a brand-new print to cut two frames of what she said was 'rear entry,' which I loved. She'd scream that out: 'Rear entry!' I never heard anybody say that in my life."

At least one other Baltimorean shared Avara's opinion of *Multiple Maniacs.* In his review in *The Baltimore Evening Sun,* Lou Cedrone inexplicably compared the film to *The Conqueror Worm* and called *Multiple Maniacs* "uglier and more repulsive than *Mondo Trasho.*"

But Waters was pleased with *Multiple Maniacs,* which he dubbed his "celluloid atrocity" and which for years he cited as his favorite among his films. The premiere, this time at downtown's First Unitarian Church—"My old showcase, Emmanuel Church, decided they had risked their necks enough for 'art,'" Waters wrote in *Shock Value*—sold out all nine of its showings.

Waters took the film with him when he returned to Provincetown in the summer of 1970, and its Cape Cod premiere was also a sellout. Back at his bookstore job, Waters got word that *Multiple Maniacs* had been picked up by the alternative Art Theater Guild, which booked the film as a midnight movie in 16 cities, including London and Los Angeles.

As Waters prepared to follow his movie around the country, the other Dreamlanders were once again wreaking havoc on Provincetown. Susan Lowe was run out of town by officials who objected to her microminiskirts ("She was showing bush!" Waters recalls) and numerous tattoos. Cookie Mueller sued the *Provincetown Advocate* when it published a photograph of her, passed out drunk, in a story about alcoholism. Divine, who was running a thrift shop called Divine Trash, had leased a posh apartment from local lawyer Carey Seamen, who was away for the summer. Broke and unable to pay his rent, Divine auctioned off Seamen's furniture to raise the funds he owed her.

Divine was rescued from ruin by an invitation to appear at the San Francisco engagement of *Multiple Maniacs*. Waters was already there, living in his car and sporting a new, pencil-thin mustache, which would eventually become his trademark. The film was doing big business at North Beach's Palace Theater, where a resident drag troupe, the Cockettes, performed before each screening. Waters wrote a live show for Divine, who arrived to a warm welcome from the adoring Cockettes.

"Before that, Divine never believed anything was ever going to come of any of this," Waters says. "He was in Provincetown without one penny, and now (someone) was sending him an airline ticket, which was really a big deal for us back then."

Waters asked his new friend Van Smith, who would go on to design costumes and makeup for all of Waters' films, to create an all-new look for Divine. Smith shaved Divine's hairline back to the middle of his scalp, "to allow more room for eye makeup," and drew on a wildly exaggerated face based on Clarabell the Clown. Divine arrived in San Francisco in a bra filled with lentils and a new black dress, and made his first-ever personal appearance before the film was shown that night. In a pair of skintight capri pants and towering heels, he pelted the audience with dead mackerel, struck glamour poses, tore telephone books in half, and threw star fits. Before leaving the stage, Divine "murdered" a local actor dressed as cop.

"Drag queens hated him," Waters says. But fans—who bought up tickets several days in advance—and critics loved him. "Divine is incredible!" enthused a DJ at local KSFX radio. "She could start a whole new trend in films."

While neither Divine nor Waters was interested in setting trends, they were both determined to become famous. Waters had already begun writing the script for his next picture, which he planned to shoot in color as soon as he returned to Baltimore. And Divine began teasing the press with hints about the film. The 300-pound drag queen ended every interview by saying, "In my next picture, I plan to eat dog shit."

Chapter Six
ON EATING SHIT

"It was a joke. The whole thing was a joke."

—John Waters

I had $12,000 to make a movie. I had to put things in *Pink Flamingos* that would get people to come see it.

—John Waters

It was all a publicity stunt of the '70s.

—Divine

It was pot humor, if only because I was on pot when I thought it up.

—John Waters

If beauty, as Jean-Paul Sartre quotes Genet, is "the art of making you eat shit," this act is the divine sacrament of Waters' black midnight mass.

—J. Hoberman, Jonathan Rosenbaum, *Midnight Movies*

The film's epilogue, where Divine eats dog shit, now ranks for some with Eisenstein's "Odessa steps" sequence and Garbo's first cinematic lines.

—*Penthouse*

Waters wanted to make the trashiest motion pictures in cinema history. And, with the final scene in *Pink Flamingos,* where Divine actually consumes dog feces, he has, arguably, accomplished that goal.

—Jamie O'Neil, *Gay and Lesbian Times*

It was hardly an improvised scene. Divine and I had been planning it for over a year. So when the day finally came to shoot it, it all seemed vaguely anticlimactic.

—John Waters

John had asked me a year before we did the scene if I would scoop up dog feces and put some in my mouth. I thought he was kidding, so I said, "Sure." A year later he said, "Well, tomorrow's your big day, you get to work with the dog."

—Divine

It was a secret. Only a few people involved with *Pink Flamingos* knew about the shit-eating-grin scene at the end of the film. John wanted to keep it quiet; maybe he was afraid some other filmmaker might beat him to it, steal the shit-pioneer award. Anyway, too much word of mouth now would deplete the surprise for the filmgoer later.

—Cookie Mueller

What the movie critics, film professors, and the uninitiated never understood was that Waters gave his people more than obvious gross-outs, like Divine's fabled shit-eating scene in *Pink Flamingos*, which was basically just a marketing gimmick.

—Jack Stevenson, *Desperate Visions:*
The Journal of Alternative Cinema

It was the first scene I thought up…something to leave them gagging in the aisles. Something they could never forget.

—John Waters

Naturally, Waters is still questioned about that scene, which draws impact from the fact that it is so obviously real.

—Fine Line Features' production notes for
Pink Flamingos' 25th anniversary

It was suggested to John that he do the take in two shots. First the dog does his duty, then cut. Replace the real shit with fake shit. Divine eats it. Cut. But John knew, we all knew, that audiences wouldn't fall for that.

—Cookie Mueller

I realized filmgoers would have trouble believing it, even without a cut. No actor could be this dedicated to cinema "art" to eat dog shit, dressed in drag, solely for the audience's amusement and entertainment.

—John Waters

John said, "No. *No.* Everybody would know we replaced the real shit for fake. Divine's gotta scoop it right up still warm off the street."

—Cookie Mueller

It couldn't be fake. It had to be one continuous shot. Turd-to-mouth, so to speak.

—John Waters

Bonnie told Divine, "Pretend it's chocolate!"

—Cookie Mueller

In the last scene of *Pink Flamingos,* I'm, well, I'm an avid dog lover.

—Divine

What else can I say about *Pink Flamingos* that the world doesn't already know? Yes, Divine ate real dog poop.

—Mink Stole

There was no question that Divine would eat the dog shit; he was a professional. It was in his script, so he was going to do it.

—Cookie Mueller

Divine's attitude was "If I puke, I puke."

—John Calendo, *Oui*

I remember the day we shot it, almost shaking from laughter because it was so weird to actually, finally see this. It was a magic, surreal day in our young lives. And Divine was a trooper. To me, it just proved what a really dedicated actor he was.

—John Waters

We fed the dog continuously for three days without letting it out for a walk. The dog's name was Nazzi, and I had been told by its owner, Pat Moran, that the dog was not exactly shit-shy.

—John Waters

It was Pat's dog, and they followed it around for hours. Apparently, all the people around made it shy. If you watch the film, you can see how unhappy she looks having to poop so publicly.

—Mink Stole

I followed the dog around for about three hours, staring at it, and the dog was having a really difficult time having a bowel movement because it wasn't used to having a camera crew following it around.

—Divine

The dog was being temperamental. I guess she realized she was now a film star; this can sometimes bring on obnoxious attitudes.

—John Waters

Finally I had to give the dog an enema so that when it did have its bowel movement it was quite runny, and wasn't what I expected. I expected a turd, and I was going to pick it up and take a bite off it and pitch the rest aside, very nonchalantly. But as it was, I had to use a scooping method and put it into my mouth. It was quite hideous and horrible.

—Divine

Divine picked up the dog shit and put it in her mouth. She chewed it, flicked it off her teeth with her tongue, gagged slightly, and gave a shit-eating grin to the camera. Presto—cinema history!

—John Waters

It was a very bitter moment that I'd rather forget.

—Divine

"Cut!" I finally yelled to the much-relieved star. I rushed over and gave her a congratulatory kiss, but I'm not sure if it was on the lips.

—John Waters

I immediately spit it out and went to a friend's house that I was having a fight with and used her toothbrush.

—Divine

I always say, if there's anything shocking about that scene, it's that at the time it was no big deal to us. It was sort of a big deal that night after it was shot. Everybody said, "Do you believe what just happened?" It was surreal, and we knew that it was a moment of absurdity.

—John Waters

It was sort of a traumatic experience for me because it was never really my scene; I'm not into shit or really into kinky stuff.

—Divine

It wasn't easy for Divine to eat dog shit. I figured it would probably taste better than health food.

—John Waters

People have always said, "Eat shit." I just showed it. I knew it would be a first and a last in movie history, no one would ever dare repeat it and no one had done it before. When people would walk out of the theater it would be the last image they would have in their mind, and they would have to remember it. It was a publicity stunt, and one that worked.

—John Waters

God, I wanted to be famous so bad, I'd wanted to be a movie star since childhood. I wanted it so bad I used to say I could taste it. Yes, I tasted it. It was hideous, and I spat it out immediately.

—Divine

Hell, I'd rather eat dog shit than read the dialogue in some of the movies I've seen recently.

—John Waters

Divine asked us, "What's the worst thing that can happen to me when I eat dog shit?"

—Cookie Mueller

That night, a distraught Divine phoned the hospital and was referred to Poisons. "Well, um, my little boy just swallowed dog feces...you know, dog doodie. How old is he? Um, he's 26. He's sort of retarded."

—John Calendo, *Oui*

Divine said the doctor didn't sound too alarmed. "I guess it's just a routine question for a doctor. He said all I have to be careful about is the white worm."

—Cookie Mueller

"*White worm?*" the cast yelled out in hysterical disbelief as Divine melodramatically grabbed his gut.

—John Waters

Divine was told that if the stomach hardened, the victim had white worm. So, for the next week, the star poked herself in the gut every 15 minutes. One day, her stomach was solid rock. "Oh, no," wailed the *cine artiste*. "This shit has finally killed me."

—John Calendo, *Oui*

At the hospital, a staff of doctors diagnosed the problem: Hysterical white worm. Unheard of—before Divine.

—John Calendo, *Oui*

Let me give you an idea of where community standards are at: When the Baltimore censor board got hold of *Pink Flamingos*, they cut out the sex and left in the shit eating. OK?

—John Waters

When Divine eats the dog shit right off the street, well, at that point a couple of people sort of began to hold their hands over their mouths and kind of started to run outside the theater, like they were suddenly in a hurry to get somewhere.

—Film critic Robert Ward

There were no laws that said you couldn't eat shit. They didn't have that on the books, so they couldn't bust it because the Supreme Court hadn't ruled whether it was obscene to eat dog shit.

—John Waters

Because of the scatological climax, even the most laid-back hippie theaters let the *Flamingos* fly only at midnight.

—John Calendo, *Oui*

In fan letters, people always say to me, "What were you? What could you have been like that you filmed this scene with eating shit?"

—John Waters

It was traumatic. I used to wake up thinking about it all the time. It was quite hideous, and not my favorite scene.

—Divine

It's one scene that will always be remembered. Divine went through 10 seconds of hell, but it was worth it.

—John Waters

Before he gobbled those turds at the end of *Pink Flamingos*, the superstar and his partners in crime were just a close-knit crowd of '60s freakos.

—film historian David Chute

My parents worried about that dog shit scene, and won't mention it. My mother said, "I won't believe that." I mean, they don't dwell on it.

—John Waters

So where can Waters go from here? How can he top a 300-pound drag queen actually eating poodle poop on-camera?

—John Calendo, *Oui*

Divine has been trying to live it down ever since, and I've been trying to live up to it.

—John Waters

Everyone always asks me what it tasted like. It tasted like shit. That's what it tasted like.

—Divine

Chapter Seven
THE SICKEST MOVIE EVER MADE

"I JUST WANTED TO MAKE A MOVIE THAT WAS BERGMAN, RUSS MEYER, AND DRIVE-IN MOVIES ALL ROLLED INTO ONE."

—John Waters

In 1997 the 25th-anniversary rerelease of John Waters' *Pink Flamingos* grossed more than a quarter of a million dollars in a modest 11-screen engagement. In 1976 the Museum of Modern Art in New York featured the film in its Bicentennial Salute to American Film Comedy. In one of its longest engagements, it played for nearly 10 years at Los Angeles' Nuart

Theatre. And, according to New Line Cinema, in its Manhattan opening weekend back in 1973, *Pink Flamingos* earned $70,188—nearly six times its teeny budget. ("I wish that were true," says Waters, who claims the film didn't gross a tenth as much its first weekend.)

Today, a quarter century after its premiere, *Pink Flamingos* continues to shock and delight audiences with its outré story and visuals. The film is routinely mentioned, along with *Eraserhead* and *The Rocky Horror Picture Show*, as the ultimate midnight movie, a film subgenre that was becoming popular in college towns across the country at the time of the film's release.

Pink Flamingos would change the lives of everyone involved with it, most notably its soon-to-be-famous writer-director, who has said, "After *Pink Flamingos,* I never had to hold a real job again." And the picture's final infamous moments, in which Divine munches a dog grumpy, would go down in cinematic history, startling a nation of filmgoers and making an instant star of the rotund leading lady.

But in the winter of 1972, few people outside of New York's film underground had heard of John Waters. He was still an unknown filmmaker, limping through the troubled shoot of his latest underfunded project.

The filming was cursed with delays and dilemmas. The rusted trailer Waters planned to use as Divine's home in the film had collapsed once they'd gotten it to the location, and he and set designer Vince Peranio had to prop it up with rotten 2-by-4s. His cameraman quit after shooting a scene in which Divine discovers that someone has mailed her a bowel movement. And despite the assistance of the "professional" camera crew Waters had hired with a portion of his scraped-together $12,000 budget, he had to scrap several days' worth of film, putting him behind schedule and costing him a bundle.

"We would shoot whole days on *Pink Flamingos* and it wouldn't turn out, because I didn't know what I was doing,"

Waters recalls. "The film jammed and came back with big scratches down the middle of it."

With most of his interior shots already in the can, Waters had been traveling to the film's primary location, a huge plot of land in Phoenix, Md., that adjoined a commune where his friend Bob Adams was living. But because the exterior scenes were being shot several hundred yards from the commune's farmhouse, the nearest source of electricity, Waters was running his lights and camera by way of a 300-foot extension cord. This less-than-satisfactory arrangement annoyed his crew, whose equipment was mostly "borrowed" from their day jobs at a local television station.

To make matters worse, Waters and Mink weren't getting along. They'd been living together in a rented house in Baltimore, which doubled as the home of Raymond and Connie Marble in the film. Preoccupied with his movie, Waters neglected his household chores, which fell to the exasperated Stole.

"Living on the set together was a strain for both John and me," Stole wrote years later. "It was probably the last time either of us ever lived with anyone we weren't sleeping with."

The other actors were beginning to bitch, too. About the freezing cold. About the lack of food. About how far they had to hike to use the john. Thank God Edie was there. She flubbed every take, but her endless supply of speed kept the cast from fleeing. Free drugs were a perk no Dreamlander could walk away from.

Drugs fueled *Pink Flamingos* from the start. "The whole movie is about pot," Waters has said. "I wrote it on pot, the audience was on pot, and when Divine said yes, he'd eat dog shit, he was on pot."

That infamous bit—in which Divine places a fresh dog turd in his mouth, gags, and smiles—was to be the last scene filmed. Waters was shooting his new movie in chronological order, partly because he had no idea where his story was heading.

"The whole script wasn't even done when we started," he says. "We did it like a soap opera, basically. I'd write a scene and we'd shoot it. I didn't know the ending in that movie; I knew the shit-eating ending, but I didn't know the actual story while we were filming."

Waters settled on a tale of two families vying for the title "The Filthiest People Alive." As Babs Johnson, Divine plays a notorious trash moll who lives in a trailer with her demented mother, Edie (Edith Massey); her pervert son, Crackers (Danny Mills); and a horny traveling companion named Cotton (Mary Vivian Pearce). Her chief rivals, Connie and Raymond Marble (Mink Stole and David Lochary), run a baby-selling business and are obsessed with Babs. To prove their filthiness, both sides perform various debaucheries, but Babs triumphs and, after a public execution of her rivals, proclaims herself God and then eats dog shit.

"The best ending of all my films was *Pink Flamingos* because it made the rest of the movie meaningless as to whether people liked it or not," Waters says today. "When people left the theater, they had to tell someone about it."

There was plenty of talk about the scene even before it was shot. According to Divine, Waters asked his leading lady, "Are you willing to take a chance? You won't have to swallow it, just put it in your mouth and spit it out. Let me get one take. If it works, you'll be a new star; if it doesn't, you'll be back doing hair or working in another junk store and never heard of again."

Several years later, Cookie Mueller wrote about *Pink Flamingos'* indulgent ensemble. "In the world there are many brave people: those who climb Mount Everest, those who work in Kentucky coal mines, those who go into space as astronauts, those who dive for pearls. Few are as brave as actors who work with John Waters. We didn't think he was asking too much. We didn't think he was crazy, just obsessed."

Not all of Waters' obsessions made it onto the screen. For one scene, he asked Stole to set her hair on fire. "In a moment of insanity I agreed to it," Stole says, "then changed my mind when I realized the only safety precaution we'd be taking was some guy standing by with a bucket of water. I'm permanently glad I didn't do it. The effect would have been totally obliterated by Divine's dining on dog poo at the end of the movie, and I'd just be bald and bitter."

Nearly two decades later, Waters would revive the scrapped scene in *Cecil B. Demented.* In that film's climactic ending sequence, Cecil asks his leading lady, played by Melanie Griffith, to set her hair on fire. The actress complies.

One scene Waters wishes he'd never filmed finds Divine performing fellatio on her son, played by Dreamland newcomer Danny Mills.

"It's the only scene I regret," he says. "If I had my way, it would be cut out. But I can't do that, because people would think the film was censored."

In a movie rife with troubling images, the blow job scene is especially hard to watch. Waters points out that the bit was meant to spoof the popularity of pornographic films, then at their commercial peak.

"That joke has been lost today," Waters admits. "People don't understand it, so it makes them uncomfortable to watch it. It makes me uncomfortable, to be honest with you."

Waters also continues to take heat over another of the film's more disturbing sequences, in which Mills and Mueller kill a chicken by squashing it between their bodies while making love. Despite criticism from even hard-core fans, the director defends the chicken scene to this day.

"Not only did the chicken get fucked, so to speak," Waters wrote in *Shock Value,* "it also got famous in a movie to boot. We actually made this chicken's life better."

In her memoirs, Mueller points out that several chickens were killed during retakes of the scene, but all were put to good use. "We roasted all those chickens and had a big feast for the whole cast and crew," she writes. "Those chickens I'd felt sorry for earlier sure were delicious."

Today, when *Pink Flamingos* is screened in revival houses, the chicken-fuck scene is sometimes deleted. Also frequently cut is the infamous "Singing Asshole" scene, in which an unnamed cast member stands on his head and manipulates his anus so that it appears to be singing. With or without the singing asshole, *Pink Flamingos* is banned on Long Island, and only much-expurgated prints of the film are allowed to play in London. But no matter where it's screened, the shit-eating scene always remains, much to Waters' delight.

Even if he hadn't eaten dog poop in its final moments, *Pink Flamingos* would have made a star of Divine. The picture provides a grotesque tour de force for the actor, whose trashy look was based on Jayne Mansfield, a favorite of both Divine and Waters. The director instructed Van Smith to design newly garish make-up that was equal parts Mansfield and Clarabell the Clown.

"We were looking for the '50s glamour girl look, gone low-brow," Smith says.

Although Smith created Divine's look, Lochary and Stole fashioned the Marbles' zany hairdos, bleaching their hair white, then coloring it—he with blue magic markers, she with Quink brand red ink.

"I would mix the ink in shampoo and wash it in each night before filming," Stole wrote many years later. "I had to be careful that it didn't stain my skin. One night I was so tired that I didn't get all the color off my neck, and in the morning I had to scrub myself with Ajax."

Peranio created a palette for Waters' first color picture that's awash in the lurid turquoise and hot pink of Waters' favorite Kuchar films. The pair scoured thrift shops and junkyards for trashy bric-a-brac to dress the set, and Waters named the movie after his favorite find: the pair of moldy plastic lawn ornaments that adorn Divine's front yard.

Those flamingos were consumed in the fire that marked the final day of shooting. With the cameras rolling, Stole and

Lochary doused the inside of the trailer with gasoline, and Stole tossed a burning torch into it. Waters' brother stood by with a tiny fire extinguisher while the actors read their lines in front of the burning set, which eventually collapsed into a heap that smoldered for days.

After the Dreamlanders returned to their nefarious civilian lives, Waters began the arduous task of editing his masterpiece. Because he believed that no movie should run longer than 90 minutes, he cut nearly an hour from the film. Entire subplots were deleted, including all of Pat Moran's scenes as Patty Hitler, a nasty tattletale who rats on Cookie the spy. Also scrapped were scenes in which Crackers and Cotton murder Cookie and her mother, as well as several vignettes from the battle of filth.

Because Waters didn't have an editing machine, he cut the film by hand, running it back through the projector over and over. "The original *Pink Flamingos* had no work print," Waters recalls, referring to the rough version of a film used to master its final edit. "I put it through (the projector) hundreds of times."

Finally, Waters looped the film's narration, a demented rant by "Mr. Jay," an off-screen character based on Mr. Ray, owner of Worldwide Hair and Beauty, a seedy Baltimore wig shop. Mr. Ray hawked his hairpieces via cheesy radio and television commercials "in one of the thickest Baltimore accents imaginable," Waters says. When the director invited the real Mr. Ray to narrate the film, the wig seller tossed Waters out of his shop.

Following its sellout world premiere at the University of Baltimore in late 1972, *Pink Flamingos* sat on the shelf for more than a year. Waters had inked a deal with fledgling New Line Cinema, a New York–based film distributor, which finally agreed to book the film for one night at Greenwich Village's 1,200-seat Elgin Theatre. The midnight screening sold out, and the film went on to play the Elgin seven nights a week for the next three years.

Waters suddenly had a hit. He wasn't surprised.

"I knew, after I saw it at its premiere in Baltimore, that I had something," he recalls. "People *staggered* out of the theater."

That something elicited an almost immediate buzz about what Fran Lebowitz, in *Interview* magazine, called "the sickest movie ever made, and one of the funniest." New Line began booking the film in art houses around the country, where management was encouraged to pass out paper sacks adorned with the logo "Pink phlegm-ingo barf bag." The distributor quickly assembled a promotional trailer that didn't utilize a single frame from the film. Instead, interviews with members of an audience exiting a *Pink Flamingos* screening were intercut with printed quotes from the film's many positive reviews.

Pink Flamingos didn't fare as well at the inevitable censorship trials that dogged the film from practically its first screening. "We usually lost," Waters says of the trials, "because in a courtroom, with 12 jurors who have never met each other and a stern-faced judge, it's obscene. It's a very unfair way to see that movie."

Waters likes to joke about the Florida family who, many years later, rented *Pink Flamingos* from their neighborhood video shop. "The parents freaked out when they saw all this depravity," he says. "They sued me, and they made the video store put my movie in the adult section. I'm *glad* I ruined that family's night."

Thirty years after its debut, *Pink Flamingos* still terrifies and delights audiences, and John Waters is still trying to live down the notoriety of creating "the sickest movie ever made."

"My biggest competition is my past," he says. "*Pink Flamingos* will always be mentioned in every review of every movie I ever make. That's OK. At least they remember something."

Chapter Eight
THE CULT OF JOHN

"I GET VERY STRANGE MAIL."

—John Waters

It's a muggy night in the downtown New Orleans arts district. Outside on the street, art enthusiasts bustle from gallery to gallery, sniffing and exclaiming about the drawings and sculptures they've just seen. Inside, I'm wedged onto a teeny sofa in the living room of one of the gallery owners, trapped between a pair of women who are noisily hyperventilating. All around us, a lively party ensues: Bursts of wild laughter erupt from the nearby buffet; snooty art fags roll their eyes at our host's newest installation; a breathtaking blond waiter serves wine.

My new companions are completely oblivious to all this. They've just met John Waters, and they're convinced that they're going to die.

I've seen this reaction before. To his fans and acolytes, Waters is a divine being. If Elvis or the Virgin Mother appeared before them, they'd consider it camp; if aliens landed in their backyard, these fans would screen *Mondo Trasho* for the little green men. Place John Waters within 30 miles of one of his more ardent admirers, and they begin panting and reciting the stations of the cross.

One of my new pals, Marcia, is trying hard not to cry. "I-can't-believe-it-I-can't-believe-it-I-can't-believe-it," she is braying, her hands tearing at the multicolored pot scrubber she's fashioned into a skirt. "It's really him! He spoke to me! I'll never be the same!"

Marcia's sister, Susan, is trying to calm her, while her niece, Amanda—a stunning beauty with chopsticks in her hair—rolls her eyes. "My aunt Marcia is a little undone," she explains to me. "We just really love John Waters."

Marcia lets out a little squeal, then bursts into tears. "We don't just *love* him," she says, dabbing at the pools of mascara collecting on her chin. "It's more than that. He has changed our lives. I remember the first time I saw *Multiple Maniacs*. I left that theater a changed girl. It took me three days to recover."

Marcia turns to Susan. "I just went in there, into that other room, and walked right up to him," she says, jerking a thumb over her shoulder. "And I said, real regular like, 'Hello, Mr. Waters.' Just like I was talking to the grocer or something. And he *smiled* at me!"

While Marcia sobs, Susan tells me that her sister is an artist, a detail that's apparently meant to explain her behavior. "Marcia feels like John Waters combines all of her personal beliefs in his work?" says Susan, whose sentences all end in question marks. "And she's never really found that before in another artist? So she's very moved by his films?"

Waters has affected Marcia's life in other ways too. "I never, ever date a man until I show him my video of *Female Trouble*," she confides later, after she's collected herself. "You can tell a lot about a person's character by how they respond to that movie. I dearly love *Female Trouble,* and I won't have anything to do with a man who couldn't sit down and watch it with me every couple of days."

One fellow didn't make it past the "birth of Taffy" scene before Marcia tossed him out. "He made a face when Divine bit off the umbilical cord, and I showed him the door," she says, scowling at the memory. "But my last boyfriend liked it so much, he asked me to rewind it and play it again. We were together for three years after that."

I notice that the tall, jowly fellow near the window, who's been eavesdropping on our conversation, looks a little queasy. As Marcia begins to describe to me how the toe-sucking sequence in *Mondo Trasho* represents the synthesis of life and art, the jowly guy blanches, then rises to leave.

As he walks past, I want to grab his arm and say, "Hey, buddy, this is nothing." I want to tell him about the woman I met who had John Waters' signature tattooed on her back, or the guy who claims his cat gives Waters the ideas for all his films. Or the teenage girl who draws on a pencil mustache with liquid eyeliner every morning before going to teach at a school for mentally retarded adults. Marcia, who is now drying her eyes with the ends of her long hair, is a walk in the park compared to some of the other Waters fanatics I've met.

Like Suki. I didn't like Suki the first time I met her—particularly after she wouldn't let me into her house. A mutual acquaintance had hooked us up, but not before warning me, "Suki is really a Waters fanatic. She can be a little scary." He told me that

Suki required anyone who visited her to bring a quote from a John Waters film, but he failed to mention that she wouldn't let you in if she didn't *like* the quote.

The first time I visited her, I came equipped with my personal favorite quote from *Pink Flamingos*—"Nobody sends you a turd and expects to live!"—but Suki sent me away.

"Do you have any idea how many people have brought me that quote?" she shouted through the closed door of her Miami tract home. "You'll have to come back another time. Sorry."

I figured she had to be kidding, and waited for her to open the door. When it became plain that she meant what she'd said, I tried reasoning with her, eventually shouting out various other quotes—"Let's all put on a folk hat and learn something about a foreign culture!" "I better get them cha-cha heels!"—through the door. But this only made her angry—especially since I'd apparently gotten some of the lines wrong.

"If you're going to misquote John Waters films, I'm going to have to call the police," she bellowed. "I'm going to bed now! Goodbye!" And she turned off her porch light, leaving me in the dark.

I telephoned her the next day and made arrangements to drop by again. This time, I came armed with an obscure and, I thought, very amusing quote from *Multiple Maniacs*.

"Nobody has been near my private parts except for this old lady I met on the bus!" I hollered at Suki's front door when I returned that evening. She apparently didn't share my amusement over this bit of dialogue—she was frowning when she opened the door—but at least I was in.

Except for the bright fuchsia bangs and the large pink flamingo tattooed on her forearm, Suki might be any middle-aged librarian or hatcheck clerk. Short and compact, she's surprisingly humorless for someone who has, as she puts it, "devoted her life to the great John Waters."

Suki's home is a testament to her devotion. Every wall of every room is covered with neatly framed and matted one-sheets and lobby cards and stills from each of Waters' feature films. I counted *Pink Flamingos* posters in four different languages and at least a dozen different portraits—in oil, acrylic, and watercolor—of Waters and Divine. Press kits from *Serial Mom, Polyester,* and *Pecker* are displayed in a glass case alongside key-chain viewers from *Female Trouble* and *Pink Flamingos* and a pile of matchbooks printed with the *Cecil B. Demented* logo. Suki's refrigerator is covered with magnets advertising the Hefty Hideaway (the fat girls' boutique from *Hairspray*), and the face of her kitchen clock is a photograph of Mink Stole.

"I have almost everything there is," she says, waving her arm to indicate the stacks of shelves and boxes overflowing with Waters souvenirs. "I need the Mexican half-sheet from *Cry-Baby* and the Beta videocassette of *Female Trouble*, a few more things like that. Then I've got it all, and I'm done."

Suki is serious about her collecting. Several times during our interview she excuses herself to "attend an auction." Seated before her laptop, she logs on to eBay, where she usually wins whatever bit of Waters merchandise she's bidding on. While I am with her, Suki bags a Portuguese *Polyester* Odorama card, an Edith Massey 45, and a can of Final Net bearing John Waters' signature, all the while screaming at the faceless people bidding against her.

"You cheesy fuck!" she shrieks when one electronic opponent dares to outbid her on a resin model of Divine dressed as a mermaid and pointing a pistol. "I'll show you 27 dollars and 77 cents!" With that, Suki places a bid of $448, which somehow drives the price up to $52.50 and wins her, with seven seconds remaining, the Divine doll, which she plans to place on her desk at work.

"I've been known to walk out of meetings to attend a John Waters auction," she says of her job as a dietitian at a local clinic. "I got bitched at by one of the supervisors for having all these John Waters posters up in my office, so I took them down and put up a note on the blank wall that said, 'If you can find some other miserable bitch to work here for shit wages with a bunch of squares, hire her.' My boss called me the next day and said, 'Come back, come back, you know I love John Waters, we need you!' Whatever. Stupid bitch says she loves John Waters, but I asked her what her favorite one of his movies is, and she said *Lust in the Dust.* I almost decked her."

Suki, who's wearing an oversize T-shirt bearing the *Cecil B. Demented* slogan PUNISH BAD CINEMA! takes me upstairs to see "the really rare stuff." Here, in her bedroom, is where she keeps the most precious artifacts of John Waters' career. "All the really good bits are up here," she confides, "locked up with me in case someone breaks in while I'm asleep."

She shows me a matted and framed flier for *Eat Your Makeup* that cost her a month's rent, a bootleg DVD of *The Diane Linkletter Story,* and a copy of Waters' high school yearbook from 1963. Above her bed, pinned like a bug in a petri dish, is a crew jacket from *Serial Mom.* But none of these items matters as much to Suki as her prized possession: a baguette autographed by Waters in 1989.

Suki can't tell me the significance of the baguette or how it came to be autographed. "How should I know?" she scowls. "Maybe he likes French bread. He was probably sitting in a French restaurant, and some asshole fan shoved a pen under his nose. So he signed this!"

Suki is not some asshole fan. She explains in great detail about what separates her from most fans, a word she disdains. "I consider myself John Waters' *archivist,*" she explains. "One day, when we're all little piles of dust, his career will be captured here in this house. Some cinephile will say to himself, 'I wonder if John Waters ever wrote his name on a loaf of bread,' or whatever, and they'll come here and the answer will be in a little glass case."

She lets out an exasperated sigh when I ask if she's ever met her idol. "No, and I'm not sure I want to. What if he turned out to be boring? I'd want to talk to him about Cookie Mueller's eye makeup, and he'd be, like, 'Seen any good movies lately?' I'd much rather *collect* him than *know* him."

Downstairs, Suki pours me a glass of water from a jug marked "Tears" and guesses that I think she's a loser.

"You probably think I'm one of those scary girls you wouldn't talk to in high school. So I dug this out when you said you were coming over." She drops a scarred scrapbook into my lap. Inside are photos depicting a teenage Suki, whose name was Deanne Newbury back then, in cap and gown, delivering the valedictorian speech at her high school graduation. In another, she's posed perkily with her pimple-faced but rather dashing prom date. In still another, she's proud captain of the "mat maids," a sort of cheer squad for her school's wrestling team.

"Deanne Newbury was the homecoming queen, the president of the senior class, and a total drip," Suki explains, in third person. "She went to her 20-year class reunion and no one had changed. Except they were all fatter. Everyone filled out these dumb questionnaires where you wrote down the biggest event of your life. Everybody wrote 'The births of my children' or some such bullshit. Deanne wrote, 'The day I saw my first John Waters movie.' People kept coming up to her saying, 'Who? Did we go to school with him?' And Deanne thought, 'I'm going to murder a cheerleader if I don't get out of here.'"

After this life-altering evening, Deanne changed her name to Suki, divorced her husband—"I only married him because he looked like David Lochary"—and began collecting. Today, she says, she has the largest collection of John Waters memorabilia in the civilized world.

She also has a shrine to him in her bathroom. Sometime in the middle of the night, during the many hours Suki has spent talking about John Waters' artistic camera placement and ingenious use of vomit and staircases, I've apparently said something that has endeared me to her. As I'm preparing to leave, she takes my hand and says, "I don't show this to just anyone."

With that, she leads me into a tiny, dimly lit bathroom under the stairs. There, fastened to the wall over the toilet, is a pasteboard altar. On it, an enormous framed oil painting of Waters rests, surrounded by tall candles and decorated with rosaries and syringes. Waters' voice, dubbed from television talk shows, plays on a continuous audio loop in the background. Suki begins lighting candles and repeating, word for word, what Waters is saying on the tape. The effect of flickering candlelight and Suki's peculiar chanting—she and Waters are saying, in unison, "I've given bad taste a good name. To me, it's good bad taste"—is enormously unsettling.

After she's lit the last of the candles, Suki sits down on the lid of the toilet. "I come in here every morning to meditate," she tells me. "I think about all the hideous things in the world and how John Waters has made them beautiful. I hated drugs and beehive hairdos before I knew his films. Now I laugh whenever I see them. And if there's anything really hideous in my life, I just sit here and think about how he would make it funny. Like the time I broke my femur and had to wear a body cast and was in constant pain. I'd wheel myself in here in the mornings and just laugh and laugh."

I've had enough, and start to make leaving noises. "Yeah, yeah, I know," Suki sighs. "Better get out now before I *really* get weird. I should get to bed, anyhow. I've got a 5 A.M. auction. Some guy's selling Sharon Niesp's dental plate, and I'm gonna win it."

Suki shows me to the door—there's a life-size, 3-D photograph of Edith Massey pinned to it—but not before giving me the names and E-mail addresses of several other Waters fanatics. Her parting shot is perhaps the most startling moment of the long evening we've spent together. "Be careful with some of these John Waters fans," she cautions. "Some of them are real nutcakes."

Those nutcakes prove to be less out-of-the-ordinary than Suki herself. I speak long-distance with Scott Lawrence, a 22-year-old Canadian whose Divine collection is posted on his Web site, The

Psychedelic Shack of Divinity. By day, Scott is a Days Inn reservations clerk; by night, he's Myra DeBoink, a girl with a big wig and a bad attitude.

"I sort of channel Divine when I'm onstage, I guess," Scott says of his nightclub drag act. "She's my idol, and really the inspiration for Myra."

Scott tells me about the John Waters Fan E-List, an electronic round robin of notes and rants by the Waters-obsessed. Moderated by a woman named Amy, the list is a folksy fan base where members chat about their favorite food scene in a Waters film or wonder what the filmmaker wears while he's in Provincetown. As a member of the list, I meet Guy Mazzaglia, a 38-year-old unemployed club DJ. For Guy, John Waters is a kindred spirit. As a kid growing up in Fort Lauderdale, Fla., Guy, like the young Waters, gave demented puppet shows and, in his off-hours, drew imaginary carnival rides that killed people.

"Everyone thought I needed medication," he says. "Then I discovered John Waters and felt this immense sense of relief. Here was a sicko who was getting *paid* for being weird."

Guy, who once got into a fistfight in a memorabilia shop over an autographed photo of Waters, shows his thanks with his Web site, TroubledWaters.com. Among fans, it's the second-most visited Waters Web site, next to Jeff Jackson's Dreamland.com, the definitive collection of all things Watersian, including an up-to-the-minute overview of the man's career.

"John Waters made me feel OK about liking both Disney movies and porno," Jeff says. "He helped me see how tragic things can be funny, and gave me a cool underdog to root for. When you're growing up gay in a small town, that's important."

Both Jeff and Guy would love to know their idol personally, and Guy, who attended film school for a while, has some "very cool ideas that John could use in his next movie."

But Waters doesn't need any new ideas, according to Earl Bolton. Earl knows this because, he says, he provides John

Waters with every one of the ideas that he uses in his films. Earl, who bears a strong facial resemblance to Paul Swift (the Eggman in *Pink Flamingos*), has no professional affiliation with Waters and swears they've never met. Earl doesn't correspond with Waters and eschews all traditional forms of communication with the man he calls "my favorite movie star director."

The way Earl tells it, he deposits story ideas in the brain of his house cat, which John Waters retrieves in a most alarming manner—even for John Waters.

"See, I got this cat named Jayne Mansfield," drawls Earl, a former public school janitor who lives just outside Albuquerque. "And Jayne is sort of what they call a familiar. She ain't really a cat, and she ain't a person. She's more like a spirit livin' inside of a cat."

Earl, who says he's a "regular fountain of good ideas, with no way to write 'em down," tells his ideas to the spirit who lives inside his cat.

"Every morning, I tell Jayne Mansfield about anything that pops into my head. I tell her about guys I knew in Nam and songs I want to write someday and people with flowers where their teeth should be. One time I told Jayne Mansfield about this place I seen once called Mortville, and then I went and rented one of John Waters' pictures and there it was: Mortville! Just like I told it to Jayne Mansfield!"

When I point out that *Desperate Living*, the John Waters movie about Mortville, was filmed years before Jayne Mansfield was born and that the movie was released to theaters long before Earl told his cat about the imaginary town, Earl's eyes glaze over.

"I told you," he says, carefully enunciating every word, "Jayne Mansfield ain't really a cat!"

Jayne Mansfield isn't the only one who isn't what she appears to be. According to Earl, John Waters is also an otherworldly being.

"I don't think he's from another planet or nothing," Earl says. "But he ain't human neither. See, he can turn himself into things, and then he hangs around and watches people, and that's how he gets his ideas for his movies and such."

Just then, Jayne Mansfield enters the room. She looks less like a supernatural being than an undernourished tabby.

Earl points to Jayne Mansfield's tail. "About once a month, John turns himself into a puff of smoke. He comes in under my front doorway there, and he goes inside Jayne Mansfield through her back door, if you know what I mean. John goes inside Jayne Mansfield's memory, and he takes out all the things I told her, ideas he can use in his movies. And he takes those ideas and he goes out her mouth in a little puff of smoke, and he goes back to Boston, where he lives."

"Baltimore," I say. "John Waters lives in Baltimore."

Earl sighs and shrugs his big shoulders. "Wherever."

"So," I say to Earl. "John Waters turns himself into a puff of smoke, and he comes here, and he enters your cat through her asshole, and he takes out all the ideas you've dictated to her, and he takes them back to Baltimore and uses them in his movies."

Earl stares at his hands for a long time before answering me. "I don't *dictate* nothing. I just tell the cat my ideas, and John Waters takes them out of the cat and he's welcome to them. I got no use for them. I don't got time to make movies here, I got things to do."

Those "things" used to include cleaning up after a lot of messy public school kids until what Earl calls "my little accident," which he describes to me three different times during the hour we spend in his cramped, filthy apartment. Ever since the accident, which has left a jagged scar across his forehead ("The kids up the street call me Harry Potter!") Earl has a hard time getting thoughts out of his head.

"I had my little accident about, oh, goin' on 12 years ago now," he tells me again. "Guy rear-ended me, and I hit my head on the dashboard of a old square-back Lincoln I was drivin'. Well, you know, ever since then, my thoughts go in circles instead of goin' up and out, like they're supposed to. Once an idea gets into my old noggin, it gets caught up in a little whirlpool and then it just keeps comin' outta my mouth over and over again. My sister says she can't talk to me no more, I'm saying the same things so much of the time."

This is the reason, Earl explains, that the same imagery—chickens and vomiting and "boys wearin' dresses"—is repeated over and over again in Waters' films.

"See, John Waters comes over here in his little puff of smoke, and he goes in and gets them ideas of mine out of Jayne Mansfield, and sometimes they're ideas I already told. But John Waters don't know I got this repeating thing, see? So that old cat says 'Girl chucks up her lunch' every time John comes, and he goes back and puts it in his movie. And so then you go rent a John Waters movie, and another one, and another one, and they all got them puking girls in them, because I was stuck."

Earl is, he explains, the man behind the giant lobster in *Multiple Maniacs*. "Couple years ago, I ate me a whole pizza before bedtime," he says, chuckling at his own recklessness. "I had a dream that night about a big old crawfish that came in and just climbed on and tried to eat me. So of course I told Jayne Mansfield about it the next day. And the next thing I know, it's there in a John Waters picture."

There's no point, I know, in explaining to Earl that *Multiple Maniacs* was filmed nearly 30 years before his crayfish dream, or that the lobster in the film was doing something other than trying to eat Divine when it climbed on top of her.

While Earl is explaining his inspiration for casting Iggy Pop in *Cry-Baby*, his sister Lucy drops by with his twice-weekly ration of rentals from the local video shop. This time she's brought *Pollyanna*, *The Trouble With Angels*, and *The Parent Trap*. "These days," Lucy explains, "Earl has a thing about Hayley Mills."

Lucy makes Earl a cheese sandwich, gives him some pills to take, and lets Jayne Mansfield out. She offers to walk me to my car, and we both say goodbye to Earl, who's transfixed by *The Parent Trap*.

Outside, Lucy eyes my portable tape recorder and notepad and says, "I'm guessing Earl has been filling your head full of nonsense."

I confess that I'm there to talk about Earl's peculiar relation to show business.

Lucy rolls her eyes and smiles. "Don't let my little brother scare you," she says. "He's harmless. All that stuff about how he's really Pee-wee Herman is just the drugs talking. Last month it was *F Troop*," she says, shaking her head and smiling. "He was going to join the army, go to war, and be on *F Troop*."

Lucy's still laughing as she drives away.

I sit in my rental car for a long time after she goes, listening to the sound of Hayley Mills playing twins through Earl's screen door. Occasionally, I can hear him hoot with laughter.

After a while, Jayne Mansfield jumps up onto the hood of the car, and we sit there like that for what seems like hours, staring into one another's eyes.

She looks like she knows something.

Chapter Nine
ISN'T THERE A LAW OR SOMETHING?

"I PRIDE MYSELF ON THE FACT THAT MY WORK HAS NO SOCIALLY
REDEEMING VALUE."

—John Waters

Pink Flamingos was a tough act to follow, and John Waters had
no intention of trying.

"I knew that if I tried to top the shit-eating scene in *Pink
Flamingos*," Waters wrote in *Shock Value*, "I'd end up being 70
years old and making films about people eating designer colosto-
my bags."

Instead, Waters decided to make a film in which the characters themselves were more shocking than what they did on-
screen. Originally titled *Rotten Mind, Rotten Face*, the movie was
inspired by the criminals Waters met while visiting his new pal,
Charles "Tex" Watson, in prison. Watson was Charles Manson's
former "lieutenant," and had been sentenced to death for his
involvement in the Tate-LaBianca murders. Waters dedicated the
film, which he eventually retitled *Female Trouble*, to Watson.

The movie's heroine, Dawn Davenport, was inspired by a
Diane Arbus photograph that Waters had recently seen of a suburban housewife with tadpole eyebrows and her hair in curlers,
holding a drooling baby. Although the film was given an X rating
and viewed by some critics as pornography, its director intended
it as something altogether different.

"I think of *Female Trouble* as Dawn Davenport just trying to get through her life, and so many bad things happen to her," Waters says. "People are jealous of her style and take her over and use her. But that's because she's really better than any of them."

The story concerns Dawn (Divine), a teenage runaway who gets knocked up and becomes a famous fashion model and terrorist. She acquires an addiction to liquid eyeliner, which she shoots directly into her veins, gets married and divorced, gives birth on a filthy sofa (biting off the umbilical cord and throwing it at the wall), has acid thrown in her face, cuts off a woman's hand, strangles her daughter, performs a trampoline act in a nightclub, shoots several people, and finally dies in the electric chair.

Female Trouble was the first film to suggest what Waters would eventually become: a keen-witted satirist with a unique take on American values. It's a stylized, more capable movie, featuring better acting and a more coherent story line than his previous films. It looks better too: Waters was working with a $25,000 budget, and as with *Pink Flamingos,* he'd hired professional cameramen to help shoot his film.

"I paid other people to use their equipment that generally was gotten quasi-legally," he remembers. "They had access to the equipment, and maybe the people who owned it—like schools—didn't know that someone was paying them to use it during off-hours."

The budget, mostly borrowed from wealthy friends, was eaten up pretty quickly—much of it by Van Smith's wild costumes. Smith laced Edith Massey into an astonishing one-piece vinyl dominatrix outfit, and squeezed Stole into giant little-girl party dresses.

"We got most of Taffy's clothes in the children's departments of the local Purple Heart," Stole remembers, "except for her Hare Krishna outfit, which was an old bedsheet dyed yellow."

Mary Vivian Pearce recalls that her costumes for the film, which was shot in sequence, become gradually less glamorous as filming progressed and funds began to run out.

"The first costume I wear, that silk suit, was made for me," Pearce says. "But the one in the hospital scene (later in the movie) is just some scarves thrown together."

Waters rented another West Side apartment, which became the new Dreamland Studios; interiors for both the Davenport home and Aunt Ida's were shot there. Exteriors were shot at the home of production designer Vince Peranio. But some locations—like the Lipstick Beauty Salon and the prison scenes, shot on an uninhabited floor of the women's section of the Baltimore jail—are real.

Smith created horrific scar makeup for Divine, who took trampoline lessons at the local YMCA to prepare for his role. Cookie Mueller was on hand as Dawn's slutty friend Concetta, and Edith Massey, always a good sport, sat in a giant birdcage for hours every day to complete Ida's scenes. Pearce and Lochary were Donna and Donald Dasher, the beauticians who brainwash Dawn and shoot her up with liquid cosmetics.

Mink Stole played Dawn's daughter, Taffy, the contemptuous brat who becomes a Hare Krishna. Stole calls this her favorite role in a Waters film, and says that Taffy is "one of the great film characters of all time." Stole elaborates, "She is based on a combination of Patty McCormack in *The Bad Seed* and John's own childhood car accident games, with more than a little of my particular brand of brattiness thrown in. It was quite interesting to realize what a good mood being an obnoxious kid on-screen put me in."

Stole says that *Female Trouble,* which remained Divine's personal favorite of his films, is the best movie Waters ever made.

"I think it's his masterpiece," she told *Mean* magazine in 2000. "There's a logic to it. The courtroom scenes are fantastic. The jail scene at the end is heart wrenching. It's a really, really well-done film."

Waters is fond of the movie too. "The first 10 minutes of *Female Trouble,* I still think, is the funniest thing in any of my movies," he says, "up to the Christmas tree, when Divine runs out the front door."

The infamous scene Waters refers to has remained a favorite with fans. Early in the film, Dawn throws a temper tantrum when, on Christmas morning, she doesn't get the "cha-cha heels" she asked for. In a rage, she stomps on the packages under the tree, hurls invective at her parents, and finally pushes her mother into the Christmas tree, which falls on top of her.

Other fans love the film for its overt gay sentiment. *Female Trouble* contains perhaps the earliest gay liberation speech in any American-made movie. In one of the film's funniest moments, Massey, as Ida, tells her nephew she wishes he would "turn nelly": "Queers are just better! I'd be so proud if you was a fag and had a nice beautician boyfriend…I worry that you'll work in an office, have children, celebrate wedding anniversaries. The world of a heterosexual is a sick and boring life."

Despite this amusing monologue, Waters was no gay activist. "The gay movement was pretty square in the '60s, until drugs came along. Drugs made gay men much hipper. I used to go to the riots because all the boys with the bombs were so cute. I was against the war in Vietnam, but I was more interested in the parties."

Following *Female Trouble*'s Baltimore premiere, Waters inked a deal with New Line Cinema, which transferred the film to 35mm for national distribution. At the time, New Line also optioned *Mondo Trasho* and *Multiple Maniacs* for release on the midnight movie circuit. *Female Trouble* became the first Waters film to play a regular engagement at a first-run theater when it premiered in New York at the RKO Fifty-Ninth Street Twin in February of 1975.

Exhibitors, concerned about the film's rude content and X rating, displayed posters which cautioned, "While designated X, preview audiences have also indicated that *Female Trouble* includes scenes of extraordinary perversity that may be seen as morally and sexually offensive." *Boxoffice* magazine suggested that, to help promote the film, theater owners should "hire fat women to stand around in the lobby."

New Line had a better idea, and hired John Springer Associates (best known for its "An Evening With…" series, a touring retrospective of faded movie actresses) to promote *Female Trouble*. Springer papered all of Manhattan with posters advertising the film, and had his publicist plant a story in *Weekly Variety* stating that Waters was looking for an "actor" who would commit suicide on camera for his next picture.

Reviews began trickling in. Judith Christ's *New York* critique read, "As vulgar and gross as the porn genre can get. Divine is marvelously funny!" The *New York Post's* Archer Winston wasn't so kind: "If you ever see John Waters' name on a marquee, cross to the other side of the street and hold your nose." But Rex Reed gave the film its most notorious and hilarious review when he wrote, "Where do these people come from? Where do they go when the sun goes down? Isn't there a law or something?"

The release of *Female Trouble* marked the beginning of Waters' long and affable relationship with the national media. The attention *Pink Flamingos* had received and its director's willingness to discuss all manner of outrageous topics—including his own homosexuality—made Waters a popular interview subject. While he'd never made a secret of his sexuality, he now had a national audience to shock with it. His candid confession in the early '70s that a gay sensibility influenced and shaped his films and his insistence that being gay was neither unpleasant nor particularly interesting were radical for the time.

"I like being homosexual, and was never ashamed of it," he told *Oui* in 1974. "It was so beautiful, and Divine, who lived right down the street, he liked it too."

Waters lamented to a *Viva* magazine writer that gay social life in Baltimore was so limited that he was toying with the idea of turning "hetero-hag." He elaborated on the concept for *Blueboy* later that year: "That's a gay person who hangs around with all straight people."

About gay romance, Waters told the same writer, "I couldn't stand to live with anybody. How could I read with somebody always nagging me? There isn't one person that I'm in love with. I find it hard to fall in love."

Waters told writer John Ives that he never denied that his films have a certain gay sensibility. "But I think black humor—not meaning racially—is first. Gay humor is a little part of that, but I've seen *Pink Flamingos* get the same reaction from bikers and drag queens. Being gay certainly led to the humor in my movies; it's part of me, so it's part of what I think is funny. But I don't think that being gay makes you good or bad. There are gay directors who are terrible."

Looking back, Waters is unimpressed with his early, forthright attitude about being gay. "I was on the cover of *Gay News* in 1973; I've been on the cover of *The Advocate*. To me, it was never a big scoop. I thought if people saw my movies, they'd figure it out."

Following two more *Female Trouble* premieres—one in Hollywood, the other at the Baltimore city jail, where one inmate hollered, "Hey, is this a *real* movie?"—the cast of the film scattered, anxious to cash in on their newfound celebrity.

Massey began making personal appearances in various cities, tap-dancing while warbling "Big Girls Don't Cry" in her demented little-girl voice. (Later in life, Edie fronted a punk band and, in her *Female Trouble* dominatrix outfit and with plastic spiders glued to her face, she toured the country as "the queen of punk" and "the mother of the Sex Pistols.")

Lochary moved to New York City, where he appeared in off-off-Broadway plays and, unfortunately, became addicted to angel dust. He died of an overdose the following year. "David's death stunned Dreamland," Waters wrote several years later, "and made us realize a whole era in our lives had abruptly ended."

Divine, convinced he was truly a movie star, moved to Los

Angeles, only to leave again for the East Coast when he was cast in Tom Eyen's *Women Behind Bars*. The off-Broadway show, a spoof of women's prison films that featured Divine as a lesbian prison matron, opened in the East Village and played through the end of the year.

"My roots are in Baltimore," Divine told *Voice Arts* magazine at the time. "I'll always go back to work whenever John needs me."

But Divine wasn't available when Waters began shooting his next feature, which he was calling *Mortville,* in 1976. The actor was appearing in a touring production of *Women Behind Bars* and, unable to break his contract, had to bow out of the film.

Waters had written the role of Mole McHenry, the former lady wrestler and botched sex-change lesbian, for Divine. Without Divine and Lochary on board, Waters decided to make a film starring only women—"sort of a berserk fairy tale about lesbians," he said at the time.

"It's a rags to riches story," Waters told *Viva*. "It's about how some people win the state lottery, and money fucks them up."

Money continued to be a real-life issue for Waters, who raised the film's $65,000 budget by forming a partnership he called Charm City Productions with his childhood camp counselor and other friends. *Desperate Living,* as the film was eventually retitled, was the first Waters film produced by an entity other than Dreamland Studios.

To compensate for Divine's and Lochary's absence, Waters began to recruit new talent. After auditioning dozens of obese women, he discovered Jean Hill, a 400-pound Baltimore substitute teacher. Hill, who made her screen debut in *Desperate Living,* had appeared in local community theater productions and occasionally did some modeling on the side. She impressed Waters right away with her bawdy sense of humor and willingness to do nude scenes.

"He made me so nervous," Hill says of their first meeting, "I went to grab for his hand, and I grabbed his dick and shook it instead."

Waters, needless to say, was delighted, and Hill won the part of Grizelda, a short-tempered, murderous domestic. Susan Lowe, who had appeared in bits in several earlier Waters films, was cast as Mole, the role originally intended for Divine.

"Sue is so convincing," Waters said of Lowe's performance at the time, "that people always assume she's that butch in real life."

In fact, Lowe looked nothing like the sour-faced bull dyke that Waters envisioned for the role. "Ugly Expert" Van Smith chopped off Lowe's long hair, bleached what was left of it white, and added prosthetic warts and scars to her lovely face.

"When Sue's children saw Mommy's new look, they ran from her in fear," Waters says.

Dreamland regulars Cookie Mueller and Marina Melin were joined by newcomer Sharon Niesp as a trio of trashy lesbians. Rounding out the ensemble cast were Pearce as the lovesick Princess Coo-Coo ("I love seeing her flouncing around with that huge powder puff, proclaiming her love for the garbage man," Stole says. "I am completely convinced she means it") and Massey as the evil queen. Waters says Massey was relieved not to be garbed in skimpy outfits, and except for the scene where she orders one of her servants to strip for her ("I hope you didn't leave no pecker tracks on my gown!") she enjoyed the role.

Liz Renay was the closest thing to a "star" to appear in a Waters picture up to that point. An ex–gun moll and former girl-friend of mobster Mickey Cohen, the 52-year-old Renay had already appeared in 24 Z-grade films (and had served a three-year prison sentence for perjury) when Waters convinced her to be in one of his pictures.

"I sought out Liz Renay," says Waters, who caught Renay's mother-daughter strip act in Boston, then followed her to Hollywood, where she'd recently been arrested for streaking down Hollywood Boulevard.

"I took her to the Brown Derby for lunch, and we signed the contract. Such a perfect cliché! It was 12 noon and she met me for lunch in a floor-length pink evening gown. I knew then that she'd work out all right."

Despite Renay's star turn and the contributions of a formidable cast, *Desperate Living* belongs to Mink Stole. Her performance as Peggy Gravel, which would prove to be her final lead role for the director, is arguably her best in a Waters picture. She goes from mad suburban housewife to princess of a criminal kingdom, shrieking, wailing, and making endless evil pronouncements along the way. Her early scenes, in which she denounces nature and accuses her own children of killing her, are riveting and enormously fun to watch.

Stole liked playing Peggy Gravel but prefers her performance in *Female Trouble*. She says of *Desperate Living,* "It always surprises me when people tell me this is their favorite John Waters film."

Waters agrees. After *Mondo Trasho,* he claims *Desperate Living* is the least favorite of his films. "It's a good film to watch if you're crashing from a glue high," he says. "But that makes it sound more negative than I feel about it. I like it, but I think it's the least joyous of my films. Maybe I was in a bad mood when I wrote it."

Desperate Living is a fractured fairy tale that takes jabs at politics, classism, and sex. It follows renegade mad housewife Peggy Gravel (Stole) to Mortville, a place populated by criminals who've eluded the law. Peggy and her maid, Grizelda (Hill), wind up there after Grizelda kills Mr. Gravel by sitting on his face. Peggy swaps her lottery ticket for room and board at the home of Mole McHenry (Lowe) and her girlfriend, Muffy (Renay). The fugitives are called before Mortville's demented Queen Carlotta (Massey), who tortures them; later, they meet her daughter, Princess Coo-Coo (Pearce), who's in love with a garbageman. When Mole wins the lottery with Peggy's ticket, she buys a sex-change operation, but Muffy doesn't like it and forces Mole to "cut it off." Peggy replaces Coo-Coo as princess, and she and Carlotta plot to infect all of Mortville with rabies. Eventually,

Mole and her cranky lesbian friends overthrow the evil queen, cook her, and feed her to the citizens of Mortville.

"I probably like it least because it did the worst at the box office," Waters says. "That always colors how I feel about one of my films, in hindsight."

Waters' opinion is probably also colored by memories of the grueling shoot, which took place over several weeks in the winter of 1976. Vince Peranio built the massive Mortville set on the grounds of an isolated farmhouse in nearby Hampstead. "It was quite satisfying to mar this idyllic country setting by creating such a terrible eyesore," Waters says. And Waters filled the town with the crowds of extras that Pat Moran and Massey had recruited ("Wanna come be in John's new movie, Hon?") at Edie's thrift shop.

"It was very, very cold," Stole recalls of the shoot. "The extras were basically held hostage. They were brought to the location on a bus, and then the bus would leave. They couldn't go inside, there was very little food. And what food there was, was bad. They really wanted to go home."

"There were days when people just would start crying from exhaustion," Waters says. "We even forgot to have food on that movie. Some of the extras got touchy about that."

Stole attempted to remedy the situation by preparing meals for the cast. Waters recalls, "Liz Renay said, 'I don't like to say anything, but I was in Terminal Island prison and the food was better than this.'"

Although she was disappointed to discover that her screen wardrobe consisted mostly of torn rags, Renay was a trooper. She didn't complain when Waters dumped cockroaches over her naked backside, asked her to smother another actor in a bowl of dog food, or told her to have a conversation with her naked breasts.

Massey flubbed her lines as usual, though she was more relaxed before the cameras and had even learned to improvise a little. During a scene where Carlotta is being mauled by one of her goons, Waters asked Massey to shout obscenities at her fellow actor.

"I told her to say, 'Rob my safety deposit box,'" Waters says, "and she said, 'Dig for gold, Daddy, dig for gold!' or something like that. I said, 'Edith, God, where did you come up with something like that?' She laughed and said, 'Oh, I just say any old bullshit!'"

Hill proved easy to work with and got on well with the rest of the cast. But she balked before shooting a scene where she and Stole make out in the back of a paddy wagon.

"She wouldn't stop fretting about having to kiss a woman," Stole recalls. "Finally, I told her to think what it was going to be like for me—her lips are bigger than my head. That made her laugh and shut her up."

After shooting wrapped, Waters commissioned what he called "a cheesy *Doctor Zhivago*–type score" for the movie, then filmed the infamous opening credits sequence: an overhead shot of an off-camera diner eating a boiled rat.

Following its Baltimore opening, New Line premiered *Desperate Living* in Manhattan. When *The New York Times* rejected display ads for the X-rated picture, which featured a photograph of a cooked rat on a plate, New Line hastily substituted new ads showing a close-up of Renay screaming.

Reviews of the film were lukewarm, and lesbians hated the film. They complained that a man had dared to make a movie about their "community" and claimed that Waters had appropriated the title from a defunct lesbian newsletter. "What kind of name was *Desperate Living* for a gay newsletter?" Waters wrote in *Shock Value*.

Although it was years before *Desperate Living* would make back its production costs, the film did big business overseas, and was especially popular in Italy, where it was heavily edited and renamed *Punk Story*. The film also did well in Germany. "They read some sort of political message into the cruel regime in Mortville holding its own citizens captive," Waters says. "They may be right. I mean, you can read anything you like into it, but

I certainly had no Marxist view. I was on the queen's side! If I lived in Mortville, I'd probably want to live with her."

In a cover story about the picture in *Take One* magazine, George Morris wrote, "With this film, John Waters has emerged into the daylight, claiming attention from a larger audience than the midnight coterie that turned *Pink Flamingos* into a million-dollar bonanza.... He wants Annette Funicello and Troy Donahue for his next film."

Instead, Waters got Divine and Tab Hunter, and a $300,000 budget, mostly provided by New Line and Michael White, who'd become wealthy producing the stage and film versions of *The Rocky Horror Picture Show*. Despite the weak box office of *Desperate Living,* Waters had established himself in the industry, and his name—mostly on the strength of *Pink Flamingos'* continuing returns—now had marquee value.

Enough value, anyhow, to convince an authentic Hollywood has-been to sign for Waters' new picture. Former movie idol Tab Hunter was Divine's leading man in *Polyester,* the film that would introduce John Waters to Middle America. Hunter, who'd reigned as a '50s heartthrob in beach party movies like *Operation Bikini* and *Ride the Wild Surf,* had spent the past 15 years playing dinner theaters. Now the 49-year-old actor found himself playing the drug-dealing lover of a 300-pound drag queen.

The movie was Waters' first to be lensed by a professional camera crew and his first to receive an R rating. Shot in wide-screen 35mm and complete with a full orchestral score, Steadicam shots, tricky split-screen sequences, and a goofy gimmick known as Odorama, which allowed audiences to smell the scents Divine's character Francine Fishpaw is obsessed with in the film, *Polyester* was a frank attempt to break out of the midnight movie mold.

"By the time I made *Desperate Living,* the era of midnight movies was over," says Waters, who wrote *Polyester* while vacationing in Provincetown in the summer of 1980.

Anticipating accusations that he'd "sold out," Waters began defending his new picture before shooting was complete. "Making a domestic melodrama with a 300-pound transvestite and Tab Hunter in Odorama is not my idea of selling out," he told journalist Seth Cagin. "I got tired of making the same movie over and over, and I figure the audience was getting tired too. I wanted to do something subtler."

He succeeded. *Polyester* is a comparatively tame John Waters film, with no foul language or nudity and no attempt to depict the unfathomable perversions of his earlier films—a fact that, in a sense, made it all the more shocking. But for mall audiences previously unaware of Waters, the sight of a giant drag queen vomiting into her handbag while a demented old lady in teenage couture looks on was still something of a revelation. While in earlier films Divine would have been found attacking an entire town with his "modeling" skills (and perhaps a sledgehammer), this time Waters smuggled him into suburbia as a frumpy housewife, a fact that more than pleased Divine.

"It was a nice change," Divine told his manager, Bernard Jay. "I was dying to get my teeth into something different—and to play the victim, instead of the person who was victimizing. At times it was scary, because I didn't know if I was doing it right, playing the underdog, when you're used to being on top of everything. It was strange but fun."

Waters was also pleased. "The role is different for Divine," he said at the time. "I was tired of him just wearing tights and being a villain."

Instead, in *Polyester,* Divine is the much put-upon heroine, Francine Fishpaw, an unhappy Baltimore housewife whose husband, Elmer (David Samson), runs a porno theater and is sleeping with his secretary. Her delinquent children provide constant anguish: Lu-Lu (Mary Garlington) runs around with "bad boys," gets pregnant, and wants to be a go-go dancer; Dexter (Ken King) is the notorious Baltimore Foot Stomper, an angel dust casualty who stomps on women's feet in grocery stores. Things start to look up when Francine meets dreamy Todd Tomorrow (Hunter), who owns the local drive-in art cinema, but it turns out that he's a drug dealer who's sleeping with Francine's evil mother (Joni Ruth White). Eventually, Francine prevails.

Polyester is a clever spoof of suburban life, informed by Douglas Sirk films like *Imitation of Life* (1959), in which the heroine is heaped with catastrophes. The story is set in a Sirk-inspired, garishly decorated tract home that was mentioned in nearly every review.

"The first day of production we had an open house for the neighborhood to come in and look at the house and the tackiest furniture we could find," Waters says. "However, we tried to make it look real, so the ones who hated it thought we liked it and didn't know what to say. And we couldn't tell them it was hideous, because maybe they had the same stuff in their house."

Vince Peranio and Dolores Deluxe filled the blue shag–carpeted Severna Park tract home with velour faux-Mediterranean furniture and ugly, contemporary knickknacks: smiley-face pot holders; poodle-shaped, crocheted toilet-paper cozies; and giant Glade solid air fresheners.

"*Polyester* is about a woman who is driven crazy by smells," Waters says. In order to bring these smells to life, cardboard Odorama scratch-and-sniff cards were handed out to theater patrons. Cued to events in the film, the cards simulated various aromas—from pizza to flatus—when audience members scratched them. The gimmick was an homage to Smell-O-Vision, a '50s exploitation fad that pumped scents into the air-conditioning systems of movie houses.

"Of course, those movies had pleasant smells, and most of our smells are unpleasant," Waters told journalists at the time.

The director says that Odorama was also inspired by Archer Winston's *New York Post* review of *Female Trouble,* in which he suggested readers hold their noses in response to any Waters film.

"After I read that, I thought maybe I should make a movie that really stinks," Waters says.

Like the film's gimmick, the characters in *Polyester* were inspired by real people. "There actually was someone like the Foot Stomper, who was arrested in Atlanta," Waters says. "The girl who wants to be Farrah Fawcett is like 50 others I'd see get off the school bus in the neighborhood where we were shooting. The husband is like some people in the movie business I've met who have literally made me shudder."

The script's comic references to abortion were inspired by Waters' hatred of the pro-life movement. "I'm pro-abortion," he says. "If you can't love your child, don't have it." The film's most-quoted line, "I'm pregnant, and I can't wait to have an abortion!" was memorably wailed by newcomer Mary Garlington.

"I will admit to a twinge of jealousy when John cast [Garlington] to play Divine's daughter in this one," says Mink Stole, who wanted the part herself. "But then I had to admit I might not have been able to pull it off a second time."

Instead, Stole was given the secondary role of Sandra Sullivan, Elmer's sex-crazed secretary. She sports skimpy outfits and Bo Derek–style cornrows in the picture.

"The cornrows were John's idea," Stole says, "but I designed the actual do. I had sex once with them in, and the next day they were all over the floor; they had scattered everywhere."

In her final Waters film, Edith Massey appears as Cuddles Kovinsky, a wacky former housekeeper who's inherited a fortune left by a past employer. After playing scoundrels in *Female Trouble* and *Desperate Living,* Massey was glad to play what she called "a nice lady" in this picture. "And I ain't so dumb in this one as I was in *Pink Flamingos* neither!" she told reporters at the time.

Other Dreamland members were on hand for cameo roles. Cookie Mueller, Marina Melin, and Susan Lowe appear as victims of the Baltimore Foot Stomper, while Mary Vivian Pearce and Sharon Niesp are seen briefly as nuns at a home for unwed mothers.

Jean Hill claims that Waters offered her $100 to appear in *Polyester;* when she refused, he made a counteroffer. "I told him, 'For $250, you can get any old fat bitch!'" says Hill, who wrote Waters an 18-page letter in which she accused him of, among other things, exploiting her.

"He swore that he would never speak to me again," Hill recalls. She eventually relented and appeared in the film as a choir member who hijacks a bus and bites a hole in the tire of Stiv Bators' car. Hill has no lines in the film.

Waters cast singer Bators, of the defunct punk band the Dead Boys, as Lu-Lu's boyfriend Bo-Bo, "the boy no mother could love." It was the first of many times Waters would hire a former rock star for one of his films. But the real stunt casting this time was Hunter.

"The first day he walked on the set of *Polyester*, I couldn't believe it," Divine told *People* magazine. "I thought, 'Tab Hunter, *here!*' He enjoyed working with me, more than he did with any of his previous leading ladies."

Divine wasn't kidding. Of his rotund costar, Hunter said, "He's super. He's like Annette Funicello gone bananas in a pasta factory. Of all the leading ladies I've known—Natalie Wood, Lana Turner, Rita Hayworth, Sophia Loren, Geraldine Page—Divine's got more on the ball than any of them."

For Waters, casting Hunter was more than just another gimmick. "I just wanted to put him in a context that you would never in a million years expect Tab Hunter to be in," the director says. "I don't think you expect to see a star from that era doing love scenes with Divine!

"He was a joy to work with, and I was real lucky, because he could have been a real prick. He basically had a good sense of humor about his image."

Divine may have enjoyed working with Hunter, but according to Bernard Jay, Divine's former manager, he wasn't getting along so well with Waters. Jay says that Divine found his director surly and impatient and that Waters shouted at his cast and demanded that they nail their scenes on the first take.

In Jay's book *Not Simply Divine,* he claims the problems began when Divine—who'd become a celebrity in his own right after touring the country with his disco act and appearing in various theater productions—demanded three times the salary Waters was offering for his services in *Polyester.* Divine also wanted a piece of the back end and billing above the title. Divine's demands were met, according to Jay, just 30 minutes before the actor was due on the set for his first day's work.

Anxious to cash in on their large investment, New Line's press release heralded Divine's performance: "Not since Davis! Not since Crawford! Not since Stanwyck or Hayward! Divine plumbs the depths of a woman's heart!"

Waters felt that his movie deserved a PG rating. "But just because it has a man playing a woman and jokes about abortion," he told a reporter, "it won't get one." He was right; the film was awarded an R rating. Regardless, the finished film garnered a good deal of mainstream attention. A New York *Daily News* headline proclaimed, "Tab Hunter is back, and a transvestite's got him!" Critics were cautiously upbeat when *Polyester* opened across the country in May of 1981.

"The acting by Hunter and Waters' Baltimore regulars really does stink, which is purposeful," according to *People* magazine, which went on to say, "*Polyester* may not be for every nose, but it smells like a hit." Even Rex Reed, who normally disdained Waters' work, acquiesced: "The hottest ticket in town is an invite to an orgy of schlock and trashy tastelessness by the name of *Polyester.*"

Divine was delighted with all the attention, and heaped praise on his childhood friend and director. "I love John," he told an *L.A. Weekly* reporter. "I've known him since I was 16 years old and I think he's brilliant. I would do his movies if we had to film them out in the cold up in Alaska, as long as he'd let me sit in a fur coat or something. He wants me for his next film, a sequel to *Pink Flamingos,* and whenever he's ready, I'm ready. How could I ever say no to the person who gave me my start? You don't go shitting on the people who've given you breaks."

But according to Bernard Jay, Divine *did* say no to *Flamingos Forever.* He objected, Jay claims, to the "sheer bad taste" of the script, which would have required Divine to, among other things, "float off to heaven on a giant turd."

Waters was having trouble securing funds for a sequel to his notorious midnight movie hit, which would have reunited Divine with Massey, Stole, and Mueller. "It was really hard to get money for that movie because it was so much crazier than *Polyester,*" he says. When Massey died suddenly from complications of diabetes, Waters abandoned the project altogether.

"I don't think you could do a sequel to *Pink Flamingos* without her," Waters told journalist Jack Stevenson. "I don't think audiences would go for a fake Edie."

Saddened by Massey's death and discouraged by his failure to bankroll a *Flamingos* sequel, Waters began work on his next film. "I'm already thinking about the next movie," he told a reporter at the time. "I'm sure I'll need a million dollars."

Chapter Ten
FAGGOTS, FAT WOMEN, AND PUKE:
The Bluffer's Guide to Recurring Imagery and Motifs in John Waters Films

"I DON'T KNOW WHAT WOULD HAVE HAPPENED WITH ALL THESE THINGS THAT ARE IN MY MIND IF I DIDN'T MAKE MOVIES."

—John Waters

With this handy guide to the recurrent themes and visuals of John Waters' films, it's possible to become a skilled Waters authority without ever seeing his movies (although you way want to watch one or two, just for the heck of it). Memorize this chapter and you can exit a revival house screening of *Female Trouble* spouting nonsense about Waters' allusions to class distinction or impress your date with insights into Waters references to Luis Buñuel and the Catholic Church. Your ability to describe Waters' use of vomit as a commentary on American culture will elevate your dilettante status, wow your friends, and lay to rest any doubts that you have far too much time on your hands.

SUBURBAN THEMES

Class Distinction
Although he claims to hate the term "white trash," Waters is clearly fascinated by the lives and personalities of lower-middle-class people. His depiction of blue-collar folks is redemptive, however: In Waters' world, these people are always more inter-

esting than their bland, middle-class neighbors. Affluent people are invariably boorish and unkind, like *Polyester*'s La Rue, who wants to be rich so she can ride around in a purple Cadillac and laugh at poor people. In *Desperate Living*, Queen Carlotta has achieved this pinnacle, and travels through her kingdom calling out to peasants, "Hi, Stupid! Hi, Ugly!"

Waters has said that his inspiration for *Pink Flamingos* came from imagining "what kind of awful people" lived in the trailer parks he'd pass on cross-country trips. The trailer-trash families in that and several subsequent Waters films are excessively calamitous people, but they're always the good guys. His villains are always wealthy or upper-middle-class suburbanites with nothing interesting to say. By the time he filmed *Pecker*, Waters' lowlifes had grown friendlier. Still, even the homeless people in *Pecker* are more interesting than the New York assholes who try to give them a makeover. In every case, Waters' class distinctions are clear: Conservative, white, heterosexual suburbanites are evil and boring, and the denizens of any counterculture are heroic and fascinating.

Suburbia

Waters further expresses his contempt for class distinction with his condemnation of suburban America. Both *Desperate Living* and *Serial Mom* begin with establishing shots of flawless suburban tract houses. But several minutes into both stories, it's apparent that the upper-middle-class people inside these homes are whacked-out and miserable. *Desperate Living*'s Peggy Gravel is seen ranting, while her husband considers having her committed and her housekeeper steals hooch. In *Serial Mom*, Beverly Sutphin's model home houses a killer—she squashes a fly over the main credits.

"Suburbia is where I ran from," Waters has said. Happily, he keeps running back in order to show us how banal and awful it really is.

The Family Unit

Waters blasts the concept of the middle-American "nuclear" family most completely in *Polyester,* with the enormously dys-functional Fishpaws: The kids are psychotic delinquents; Dad's a pornographer; and Mom's a 300-pound man in a dress.

Elsewhere in his films, Waters represents self-made families: gangs with a common goal who move together in a pack, usually with Divine as the "parent." In *Multiple Maniacs* she's head of the Cavalcade of Perversion, with Mr. David as the father and the sideshow freaks as their children. In *Cry-Baby,* a movie lousy with orphans, the Drapes form an unusual family unit, as do the Sprockets in *Cecil B. Demented.*

The Generation Gap

The melodramatic argument between Diane and her parents in *The Diane Linkletter Story,* in which Diane tells her parents she wishes she were pregnant and proudly announces that she's on LSD, predates similar scenes in *Female Trouble,* where Dawn Davenport dumps a Christmas tree on top of her parents, then flees, and *Cry-Baby,* where just before running away Wanda Wood tells off her parents. These scenes mirror the fights the teenage Waters had with his parents. The theme is merely a microcosmic commentary on Waters' us-versus-them philosophy, which pits establishment types (in this case, parents) with freethinkers (freewheeling teens).

RELIGIOUS THEMES

Catholicism

Waters was raised Catholic and attended a Christian Brothers high school, and the Catholic obsession with suffering has heav-ily colored his view of the world. His films are rife with references to the Bible, both literal (Christ's Crucifixion in *Multiple*

Maniacs) and figurative (Divine declares herself God in *Pink Flamingos*). He often includes saints and other biblical personalities (the Infant of Prague in *Multiple Maniacs*) and occasionally goes in for outright sacrilege (the notorious "rosary job" in the same film).

Churches appear in *Multiple Maniacs* and *Serial Mom;* nuns appear in *Roman Candles, Hairspray,* and *Polyester.* The heroine of *Polyester,* Francine Fishpaw, is a champion Catholic: She prays for her husband's sins and later sends her daughter to the Home of the Shepherd's Flock, a Catholic home for unwed mothers.

Pink Flamingos contains obscure references to the Holy Trinity: After Divine declares herself God, both Cotton and Crackers repeat the sentiment aloud. Crackers lives in a shack that might be considered a manger, and his name is slang for a communion wafer, which represents the body of Christ. Which makes sense because, if Divine is God, then her son, Crackers, would be the son of God.

Then again, maybe not.

Religious Fanaticism

Waters is fascinated by religious fanaticism: During the "rosary" scene in *Multiple Maniacs,* Mink mentions 24-hour prayer sessions; in *Mondo Trasho,* Divine laments, "I can only pray so hard!" and in *Cry-Baby,* Milton's parents say they prayed so hard they got headaches.

The Virgin Mary

Probably because she's human, Waters is fascinated with the Mother of God. Next to *Pecker,* in which she appears in the form of Memama's miraculous plastic statue of Mary, *Mondo Trasho* is his most Mary-centric film, though there are also references to Mary in *Multiple Maniacs,* in which she's portrayed by Edith Massey, and *Polyester.* Waters has written about the Virgin in *Crackpot* (his "Hail Mary" essay, in which he dishes Jean-Luc

Godard's film of the same name) and depicted her in his photography exhibits (in the hilarious *Seven Marys* piece, in which the seventh Mary is Paul Lynde). Waters likes Mary because she's famous, sexually abstinent, and a symbol of motherhood, which he loves to spoof.

OTHER PREDOMINANT THEMES

Teen Pregnancy, Abortion

Both for their shock value and aggressive antichurch stance, teen pregnancy and abortion turn up often in Waters films. In *Polyester*, Lu-Lu, who is two months pregnant, announces, "I'm getting an abortion, and I can't wait!" In *Cry-Baby* teenage Pepper is "all knocked up" with her third baby, while Lenora claims to be carrying Cry-Baby's child. And then there's *Female Trouble's* pregnant teen runaway, Dawn Davenport, who refers to her grown daughter as "an abortion" and whose girlfriend Concetta cries, "I'm glad I had an abortion!" And, of course, the title character in *The Diane Linkletter Story*—who shrieks, "I wish I was pregnant!"— predates all of these. Also, the name "Dr. Coat Hanger" in *Mondo Trasho* is a reference to back-alley abortionists who used coat hangers as makeshift medical tools. More abortion humor can be found in Waters' "Hatchet Piece" essay in *Crackpot*.

Rock and Roll

Rock music has a high profile in Waters films. His early soundtracks—particularly *Mondo Trasho*—are bursting with obscure rock-and-roll B sides. He employs rock stars—Sonny Bono, Debbie Harry, Iggy Pop, Stiv Bators—as actors, and uses rock and roll as a primary plot point: *Hairspray's* Tracy Turnblad dances on a pop music TV show, and *Cry-Baby's* lead character fronts a rock band. Waters is recalling rock's early, bad-boy image in these stories.

Fame

Fame and notoriety are one and the same in John Waters' world, and his people fall into three basic categories: those who have been elevated to infamy before we meet them (Divine in both *Multiple Maniacs* and *Pink Flamingos*); those who are in search of fame (Dawn Davenport in *Female Trouble* and Cecil in *Cecil B. Demented*); and those who become famous by accident (Tracy Turnblad in *Hairspray*, Beverly Sutphin in *Serial Mom*, and Pecker in *Pecker*). In two of his earliest films, Waters depicts celebrities: Jackie Kennedy (*Eat Your Makeup*) and Art Linkletter (*The Diane Linkletter Story*). In *Serial Mom*, Suzanne Somers plays herself. The acquisition of fame is a universal desire, one that makes Waters' characters appear more like us and therefore more accessible—even when they're murdering people, raping chickens, and doing other things that most of us wouldn't.

Caught in the Act

From the time *Pink Flamingos'* Raymond and Connie Marble discovered their butler wearing Connie's clothes, Waters has depicted people getting caught doing embarrassing things. In *Multiple Maniacs, Female Trouble,* and *Polyester,* Divine catches her husband with another woman; in *Desperate Living,* Peggy discovers her children playing doctor; in *Polyester,* Divine's mother walks in on her while she's on the toilet; and in *Serial Mom,* Scotty is caught masturbating. Waters' message is directed at the audience: As cinemagoers, we're voyeurs who've invaded the privacy of the people on-screen, and consequently we are just as culpable as the intrusive characters in the films.

Audiences

Waters essentially divides the world into voyeurs and exhibitionists. While both fascinate him, he tends to side with the exhibitionists—probably because he is, as a filmmaker, one himself. Audiences in Waters movies are often portrayed as bloodthirsty and grotesque. In his first feature, *Mondo Trasho,* the freaks in the mental hospital become violent when, after watching Mink Stole tap-dance, they line up to rape her. In *Female Trouble* and *Multiple Maniacs,* that trend is reversed when Divine attacks audiences who have come to see her "perform."

Two other noteworthy audiences turn up in *Multiple Maniacs:* the suburbanites at the Cavalcade (seen as judgmental snobs who deserve what they get); and the even scarier group that gathers at the end of the movie to cheer as the National Guard kills Divine.

Capital Punishment

Waters is against capital punishment, which he comments on repeatedly in his films. Most notably, there's the chicken-killer dressed as a medieval executioner in *Mondo Trasho* (an absurdist comment on this primitive and outdated means of punishment), and the execution of Dawn Davenport in *Female Trouble.* Other references to capital punishment appear in *Pink Flamingos, Desperate Living,* and *Serial Mom.*

Nature as a Force of Evil

Waters loves to take beautiful pastoral settings and defile them with scary attacks on nature. In *Mondo Trasho,* Bonnie visits a lovely park overrun with cockroaches. In *Polyester,* Francine is attacked by both ants and a skunk in the picnic scene. For the definitive Watersian take on nature, see Peggy's "trip to Mortville" scene in *Desperate Living,* in which she wails, "All natural forests should be turned into housing developments!"

SEXUAL THEMES

The Sex Act

Waters, who claims to like sex, always makes the act appear ludicrous and ugly in his films. In *Pink Flamingos,* Raymond and Connie suck one another's toes in bed. In *Female Trouble,* Dawn

Davenport has sex in a garbage dump and later has a carrot shoved into her mouth during marital relations with Gator. Sex is often perverted, as with Mink's "rosary job" in *Multiple Maniacs,* or highly fetishized, as with the foot-stomping Dexter in *Polyester.* Sex is always at least embarrassing: Witness the Sutphin children's horror at the sounds of their parents' lovemaking.

It's hard to find a Watersian sex scene that doesn't include incessant chatter throughout; his people are forever discussing a murder plot or at least cheering one another on while fornicating.

Sex is not pornographic in a Waters movie, because his people are sexual degenerates. His films laugh at sex rather than champion it. His message: Heterosexuality and procreation are silly.

Homosexuality
Presumably because he's gay, and certainly because homosexuality is a social taboo, Waters makes films that are rife with queers. Neither *The Diane Linkletter Story* nor Waters' early silent films contain gay characters, but his middle-period films all include at least peripheral gay characters. They are always colorful and successful people and are never tormented by their sexual orientation. Waters' gay people are never villainous *because* of their homosexuality; a baddie who happens to be queer—the murderous Mink in *Multiple Maniacs,* for example— is just that.

There are few or no gay characters in Waters' later films, except for *Cecil B.Demented* and *Pecker,* which is crawling with homos: Mr. Nellbox, the lesbian strippers of the Pelt Room, the patrons and go-go boys at the Fudge Palace, and others. Even when there are no homosexuals in the story, Waters films are bursting with gay sensibility and queer aesthetic, and there are gay actors in every scene. Usually Waters casts gay people as heterosexuals and hands gay roles to his straight performers, further subverting the issue of sexuality in his films.

Heterosexuality

In John Waters films, straight people are often depicted as stupid and boring, their lives banal and unsatisfactory. In *Desperate Living,* Peggy Gravel's life becomes more colorful after she escapes the doldrums of suburban family life and has an affair with her maid, Grizelda. *Pecker*'s sister risks alienation from her family to work in a gay bar because she prefers the company of men who are "light in the loafers."

Waters' opinion of heterosexuality is best summed up by the final line of a speech given by *Female Trouble*'s Ida (Edith Massey): "The world of a heterosexual is a sick and boring life!"

The Prowling Pervert

In *Mondo Trasho,* the Shrimper trails Bonnie through the park; in *Pink Flamingos,* Raymond Marble flashes unsuspecting passersby; in *Serial Mom,* Marvin Pickles spies on strangers in public rest rooms; in *Polyester,* Dexter hunts women's feet. Waters' affection for lurking, sex-obsessed sickos is a commentary on our pernicious interest in the sex lives of others.

Foot Fetishism

It's not feet that excite John Waters, but the ludicrousness of foot fetishes. *Mondo Trasho* contains close-ups of Mary Vivian Pearce's feet in high heels, a shrimping scene, and a retelling of Cinderella—the ultimate fairy tale for foot freaks. In *Multiple Maniacs,* Cookie is introduced feet first, as is Divine in *Pink Flamingos.* In *Polyester,* Dexter achieves pleasure by stomping on women's feet.

CRIME AND CRIMINALS

Drugs

Drugs are high on the list of social taboos that Waters celebrates in his movies. In *The Diane Linkletter Story,* Divine gleefully snorts coke and smokes grass over the opening credits; later, Diane comes home stoned on LSD and commits suicide. In *Mondo Trasho* and *Multiple Maniacs* we watch men shoot heroin. Also in *Multiple Maniacs,* Bonnie tells Mr. David that having sex with him is better than amyl nitrate, and a junkie in need of a fix is presented as entertainment in the Cavalcade of Perversions. *Female Trouble*'s Dawn Davenport mainlines liquid eyeliner. And in *Hairspray,* Pia Zadora implores Tracy and her friends to "get naked and smoke" marijuana.

Shoplifting

One of Waters' favorite pastimes as a youth, shoplifting first turns up in *Mondo Trasho* when Divine steals a dress from the Hadassah Thrift Store and then swipes a pair of shoes from a drunk. Shoplifting is most fully explored in *Pecker.*

The Media and Criminals

From his first feature, Waters has explored the symbiotic relationship between criminals and the media. In *Mondo Trasho,* Divine is confronted by a reporter from *The National Enquirer,* whose voice is dubbed by Waters himself. The reporter knows that Divine is a criminal, but treats her like a star and keeps repeating, "Great, great!" as she speaks.

Waters stages a press conference—either planned or impromptu—in nearly every one of his movies, beginning with *Mondo Trasho* and continuing through to *Cecil B. Demented,* which in some ways is a series of guerrilla press conferences.

In *Female Trouble,* Donald and Donna Dasher are stand-ins for the media, which exploit crime and depravity for profit. They help turn Dawn into a media star and inflict her on a thrill-hungry audience, not unlike what Waters himself did, in a more benign way, with Divine. As a filmmaker, Waters is part of the exploitative media who, like the Dashers, played up the hideousness of his Dreamland stars in order to achieve fame and success.

He's both an exploitative huckster and an artist commenting on the same.

LIVING THINGS

Rats

Beginning in Waters' later films, rats are used to disrupt otherwise pleasant situations. In *Hairspray* a romantic insert of the moon reflected in a puddle is spoiled when a rat runs through the shot; in *Cry-Baby* our hero's jailbreak is foiled by a mirthful sewer rat. And of course there's Waters' most notorious use of the filthy rodent: Over the opening credits of *Desperate Living,* a boiled rat is served on fine china. In *Pecker* rats are briefly redeemed: Pecker's photograph of two rats screwing in a garbage can helps him achieve fame.

Birds

In *Serial Mom,* a film in which a character is even named Birdie, Beverly is obsessed with birds: She mimics their calls, reads books about them, and plans birdwatching excursions. In *Desperate Living,* Queen Carlotta offers pizza to a sparrow and has a daughter named Coo-Coo (cuckoo). In *Female Trouble,* Ida is trapped in a giant birdcage. And let's don't forget that in 1972 John Waters made a movie called *Pink Flamingos.*

Chickens

OK, chickens are birds too. But since (next to vomit) chickens are Waters' best-known motif, they get their own subsection. Waters claims to have been terrified by chickens as a child, which probably explains his ongoing use (and abuse) of them. *Mondo Trasho* begins with a man in executioner's garb beheading chickens. Then there's the famous chicken-fuck scene from *Pink Flamingos.* In the television edit of *Cry-Baby,* Lenore tosses a live chicken onstage while Baldwin and his crooner pals perform a song called "Chicken." In a particularly frightening scene from *Serial Mom*, the Sterners eat a chicken dinner.

The chicken is a symbol of rural, hayseed life, so Waters' fascination with fowl may be a reference to the hillbillies he so admires in his early work. And according to Freudian dream analysis, chickens represent the fear of being abused by others, another recurring theme in Waters films.

Dogs

Waters expresses his distaste for dogs in both his essays and his films. Dogs turn up as questionable and creepy in *Polyester, Desperate Living,* and *Serial Mom.* In *Multiple Maniacs,* Mr. David and Lady Divine are involved in "poodle-napping."

TERRIBLE THINGS

Vomit

Puke is among the most consistent visuals in Waters' films. "Ingmar Bergman really influenced me by his dramatic use of realistic regurgitation," he has said. In *Mondo Trasho,* Dr. Hanger's nurse vomits when she sees Bonnie's monster feet. In *Pink Flamingos,* Susan barfs at the site of Channing impregnating her cellmate with a syringe. In *Female Trouble,* Taffy's drunk father (played by Divine in "male drag") ralphs on her. In *Desperate Living,* Muffy blows chunks when she sees Mole's sex change. In *Polyester,* Francine heaves into her handbag at a fancy dress shop. In *Hairspray,* Amber boaks on the bumper cars. In *Pecker,* Little Chrissy projectile vomits a Ritalin tablet. Probably Waters' most famous barf reference is the infamous Puke Eater in *Multiple Maniacs.*

All this cookie-tossing serves two purposes in Waters' world. Puking is a commentary on Middle America, which presumably finds the acts Waters depicts in his films inexcusable and stomach-wrenching. Mostly, though, vomiting provides an unforgettable visual—one of the filmmaker's favorites—that always gets a loud audience response.

Reading Material

Waters, a voracious reader, uses books and magazines to establish characters and as a visual gag. In the opening segment of *Mondo Trasho,* we see Bonnie reading Kenneth Anger's *Hollywood Babylon* on a bus, and Waters has managed to wedge at least one shot of someone reading an unusual book or magazine into every one of his films since. In *Desperate Living,* Princess Coo-Coo is seen reading a romance comic. In *Polyester,* Lu-Lu is discovered reading *Farrah's World,* a biography of Farrah Fawcett-Majors. In *Hairspray,* Penny reads *Black Like Me,* and Pia Zadora reads passages from Allen Ginsberg's "Howl." In *Serial Mom,* Beverly Sutphin owns several scary books, among them *Helter Skelter,* and her nighttime reading is usually a biography of a famous serial murderer. Elsewhere in that film, Birdie is found reading a biography of Mahatma Gandhi. At the beginning of *Pecker,* a big woman is shown reading a copy of *Fat and Furious.* Other literary references never made it to the screen. In a scene excised from *Pink Flamingos,* Crackers and Divine read aloud from *Midnight,* and in the published script for *Flamingos Forever,* Baby Divine reads *The Three Little Pigs.*

Garbage

Because Waters' films are often figuratively referred to as "trash" and "garbage," he sometimes points his camera at actual refuse, thus staying one step ahead of his critics. In *Mondo Trasho* the credits are superimposed over a shot of open garbage cans; in *Desperate Living* most of the main characters live in a town made entirely of trash.

Staircases

Perhaps influenced by filmmaker Douglas Sirk, Waters often uses staircases for dramatic purposes. In *Mondo Trasho* much of the action in the Cinderella sequence takes place on a staircase. In *Female Trouble,* Dawn gives a speech about divorcing Gator while standing on a staircase. Other angry staircase speeches are delivered in *Multiple Maniacs* and *Desperate Living.*

Assholes

Other than the foot, no part of the body is more important in Waters' movies than the anus. The word "asshole" is obviously his favorite profanity, and he's used it in just about every movie he's ever made. It's used to describe anyone who is behaving badly, as when Divine convicts the Marbles of "assholism" in *Pink Flamingos.* Mink Stole has the dubious honor of being the first person to ever utter the word "asshole" in a Waters film; she uses the epithet to describe Mr. David in *Multiple Maniacs.* Mink will later tell Sandy Sandstone in *Pink Flamingos* that there are only two kinds of people in the world: her kind and assholes.

Waters' favorite curse word is uttered in *Cry-Baby* by Willem Dafoe; Matthew Lilliard gets the honors in *Serial Mom;* and Christina Ricci continues the proud tradition in *Pecker.* But nothing tops the most obvious and overt display of all things anal: the infamous Singing Asshole in *Pink Flamingos.*

TRANSPORTATION

Automobiles as Deadly Weapons

Killer cars are a Waters staple. This motif is found in *Mondo Trasho,* where Divine runs over Bonnie with a Cadillac, and *Polyester,* where Francine meets her future boyfriend Todd Tomorrow at a fatal accident. In *Multiple Maniacs,* Mr. David recalls that Divine killed a cop by running him over, the same method Beverly uses in *Serial Mom* to kill her son's teacher. In both films, the victim is described as having been flattened "like a pancake."

The Bus

In his films, the bus is Waters' transportation of choice. It's easy to see why: Buses tend to bring a varied group of oddballs together in an enclosed space and are a low-rent, low-income form of public transportation. Buses appear in both *Pecker* and *Mondo Trasho* (where the two gossipy ladies at the end of the picture are seen waiting for a bus). In *Multiple Maniacs,* Divine and Mink Stole discuss murder on their way to a bus stop.

Waters has said that people on buses must be fantasizing about sex because they all look so bored.

The Paddy Wagon

Waters often has his main characters tossed into the back of a paddy wagon—both for dramatic effect (there's definite drama in having a character dragged, kicking and screaming, into one of these infamous vehicles) and because it's such a corny cliché. Paddy wagons appear in *Cry-Baby, Cecil B. Demented, Hairspray,* and *Desperate Living.*

Car Fetishism

In *Crackpot,* Waters writes that he drives plain-looking cars and can't stand flashy convertibles. Maybe that's why Divine drives a Cadillac convertible in both *Mondo Trasho* and *Pink Flamingos.* In *Polyester,* Tab Hunter, who's very uncool, drives a Corvette with leather seats, whereas in *Cry-Baby,* the very cool title character eschews automobiles altogether and rides a motorcycle.

PEOPLE

Men

Waters tends to depict men as despicable and unequipped to provide for their partners and families. This is a popular position among feminists as well as homosexuals, who feel abandoned by an iconic masculine society.

Men as Milquetoasts

The male characters in Waters' films are either completely worthless or subservient to strong women. Waters' milquetoasts include *Multiple Maniacs'* Mr. David, who is Lady Divine's toady; Raymond Marble in *Pink Flamingos,* who clearly defers to his powerful wife, Connie; and Eugene Sutphin, who lives in a world almost entirely run by his wife, Beverly, in *Serial Mom.*

Men as Infidels

To prove their utter worthlessness, Waters' men are notoriously unfaithful, usually to Divine: In *Polyester* her husband, Elmer, is sleeping with his secretary, and later we learn that her boyfriend, Todd, is screwing her mother. In *Multiple Maniacs* her lover, Mr. David, is sneaking around with Mary Vivian Pearce. The man who impregnates her in *Female Trouble* tells her to go fuck herself; later, she catches her husband in bed with a tart. Even poor Bonnie, *Mondo Trasho's* leading lady, is abandoned by the Shrimper, who crawls off after he's sucked her toes, presumably to molest another unsuspecting girl.

Men as Sex-Toys/Providers

At best, Waters' men are a stupid, sexy means to an end; at worst, they're a necessary evil. Whether using men to father children (as with Pepper's Milton in *Cry-Baby*), to complete the perfect domestic picture (as with Beverly's Eugene in *Serial Mom*), or to provide a quick ride to the local theme park (as with Toe Joe in *Cry-Baby*), men are pets and providers. Mostly they provide fortification and sex, as demonstrated by Queen Carlotta's goonish footmen in *Desperate Living.*

Women

Women as Supreme Beings

Waters' world is a matriarchal one. His female characters rule their lives and the lives of their men, most of whom are spineless wimps. Worthless or not, many of Waters' men seem to have been raised by single women, and never by single men. Even Pecker, who has a father, is ruled by the women in his life: Memama and her Mary statue; his domineering girlfriend, Shelly; and his manipulative agent, Rorey.

In *Cry-Baby*, Mrs. Vernon-Williams is the pillar of her community and, like Lady Divine in *Multiple Maniacs* and Connie Marble in *Pink Flamingos*, runs her own successful business where men are either nonexistent or mere employees. Divine is an unapologetic single mom in *Multiple Maniacs*, *Pink Flamingos*, and *Female Trouble*. *Desperate Living*'s Mortville is overseen by Queen Carlotta, who is attended by exclusively male servants. And the treacherous plots of *Polyester* and *Serial Mom* are engineered by strong women (LaRue and Beverly, respectively) who use men (Todd Tomorrow and Eugene) as their foot soldiers.

With the exception of *Cecil B. Demented*, *Pecker*, and arguably *Cry-Baby*, in which the title character is notorious but not famous, all of the people who achieve fame in Waters' stories are women: Lady Divine in *Multiple Maniacs* and *Pink Flamingos*; Dawn Davenport in *Female Trouble*; Tracy Turnblad in *Hairspray*; and Beverly Sutphin in *Serial Mom*.

Women create stronger, longer-lasting bonds during times of crisis, as with Peggy and Grizelda in *Desperate Living* and Francine and Cuddles in *Polyester*. As Waters sees it, women are more capable and infinitely more interesting than men.

Women as Born-again Lesbians

Lady Divine in *Multiple Maniacs* is the first Waters heroine to become a lesbian after a heterosexual relationship turns sour. *Desperate Living* contains two more in the characters of Muffy and Peggy. Dawn Davenport winds up a lesbian in *Female Trouble*, and Babs Johnson declares herself a lesbian in *Pink Flamingos*, even though her only sex in the movie is with her son.

Fat Women

Jean Hill, Ricki Lake, Edith Massey, and Divine were all bigger-than-life leading ladies in Waters' early- and middle-period films. He admits that Fellini, who also used a lot of hefty women in his films, was an inspiration. Saraghina in Fellini's 8½, the portly mother in Tony Richardson's *The Loved One,* and the legion of busty gals in Russ Meyer's films further influenced Waters' taste in flabby female stars. It's easy to interpret his interest in fat women: Obesity is an indication of excess, something Waters lives for, and fat people provide big, screen-filling personalities to boot. Besides, there are certain grotesque and unclean qualities—both themes Waters holds dear—attributed to being overweight.

Today, with Edith and Divine dead, Jean Hill in ill health, and Lake sporting a newly slim talk-show-host figure, Waters seems to have lost interest in big gals and is flaunting other forms of excess.

Mad Housewives

Long before *Serial Mom*'s Beverly Sutphin, Waters delighted in the popular '60s notion of housewives gone berserk. Both Peggy and Muffy in *Desperate Living* are upper-middle-class wives and mothers who murder their husbands, and both utilize unusual weapons that are symbols of their bourgeois existence—Peggy uses a bottle of Chanel No. 5 and her housekeeper, while Muffy kills with a bowl of dog food and the power windows on her expensive car.

PLACES

Baltimore

Waters attributes his fascination with Baltimore, where all his stories take place, to the city's "extreme style." But his interest in his hometown is always in its seedy side, its downtown dives and more squalid citizens. To Waters, who was raised in moderate affluence, Baltimore's lower class is glamorous because it subverts the upper-middle-class values he was raised with.

His stance might be seen as classist (rich white kid obsesses on poor white trash) or exploitative (Waters' films have been called "freak shows" by some critics), but his vision of Baltimore and its denizens is ultimately joyous. His dismissive approach to his privileged background might be construed as a childish, over-extended teen rebellion but for the fact that his heroes are always underprivileged Baltimoreans. Waters' affection for Baltimore is real, though one suspects that if he'd been born in Detroit, his films would aggrandize the hillbillies of that city's neighboring burgs.

Reform School

Parents are forever threatening their teenage daughters with reform school in Waters' pictures—usually because the girls are dating some thuggish boy. Usually, like Coo-Coo in *Desperate Living* and Diane in *The Diane Linkletter Story*, the girl sneaks off to see the boy anyway: Both Penny in *Hairspray* and Lu-Lu in *Polyester* climb out of their bedroom windows to see their forbidden lovers. This motif mirrors Waters' real-life banishment from longtime best friend Mary Vivian Pearce when they were teens.

Actual reform schools appear in both *Polyester* and *Cry-Baby*.

Mental Hospitals

Waters' characters are forever being carted off to nuthouses or threatening to send one another to the loony bin. The asylum in *Mondo Trasho* is a snake pit, and in *Hairspray*, Waters himself plays a wacko psychiatrist. All of this suggests the filmmaker's tremendous distrust of the mental health industry.

FILMIC INFLUENCES

Old Hollywood

Waters loves to spoof the old Hollywood cliché of giving "character billing" to an actor or actress in lieu of top billing. Usually, Waters mentions his movie's most shocking or ludicrous role in the opening credits as an "And…as…" credit, just to bag a cheap laugh. The tradition began with *Mondo Trasho,* with the billing, "And introducing John Leisenring as 'The Shrimper,'" and continued in *Multiple Maniacs* with, "And George Figgs as Jesus Christ." By the time of *Cry-Baby,* the "and…as…" credit has been reduced to the rather innocuous "And Polly Bergen as Mrs.Vernon-Williams."

Final Freeze-frame

Waters' films usually end with a freeze-frame close-up of the main character. In his early pictures, this constituted what Waters scholar Joe Blevins calls the "Dead Divine Shot": *The Diane Linkletter Story, Multiple Maniacs,* and *Female Trouble* all end with a close-up of Divine's character at the moment of her death. Waters likes to end his movies showing the face of the main character and, without Divine to kill, he's lately been opting for goofy freeze frames instead. These occur in *Cry-Baby, Pecker,* and *Serial Mom.*

Animated Disney Features

Waters claims that Disney's animated films, particularly *Cinderella* and *Snow White and the Seven Dwarfs,* are among his all-time favorite movies. Bitchy women dressed as *Snow White*'s Evil Queen (whom Waters idolized as a child) appear in *Desperate Living* (Peggy Gravel) and *Cry-Baby* (Hatchet Face). The Cinderella story—in which a poor woman becomes wealthy or is reclaimed in some fashion—recurs in his films: In *Desperate Living,* Mole McHenry wins the lottery; in *Polyester,* Francine is rescued (if only temporarily) from her horrid life by handsome prince Todd Tomorrow. In *Mondo Trasho* (and in Robert Maier's Edith Massey biopic, *Love Letter to Edie*), the Cinderella story is enacted literally, as a fantasy sequence.

The vivid colors and cartoonish characters in Waters films are defiantly Disneyesque, and the theme parks in *Hairspray* and *Cry-*

Baby recall the garishness of Disneyland. And as in many animated Disney features, people interact with animals as if they're people: *Desperate Living*'s Queen Carlotta is visited by a bird, who lands on her windowsill while she's having lunch; a rat helps Cry-Baby with his jailbreak, then laughs maniacally when he tunnels his way back into prison.

In an odd turnabout, Disney referenced John Waters with Ursula, a character clearly based on Divine, in *The Little Mermaid* (1989).

Other Filmmakers

Delmer Daves

Hollywood screenwriter Daves turned director in 1943 with the classic *Destination Tokyo* and is best remembered as the creator of high-gloss soapers like *An Affair to Remember* (1957), *A Summer Place* (1959), *Parrish* (1961), and *Rome Adventure* (1962). The overacting and sexual subtext of these late-period Daves flicks, in which trampy girls get pregnant by losers and end up with humpy Troy Donahue in the end, is evident in Waters' own teen-angst films, most notably *Cry-Baby*. Waters counts Daves' *Susan Slade* (1961) among his favorite movies.

William Castle

The smelly Odorama cards issued at screenings of *Polyester* are an homage to Castle, whose screen gimmicks are more memorable than most of his movies. Stunts like "Percepto," "Illusion-O," and "Emergo" (which flew a plastic skeleton out into the audience on a wire) made Castle famous. His movies are a lot of fun, particularly the later ones in which an aged Joan Crawford became Castle's new gimmick. References to the Castle-Crawford epic *Strait-Jacket* (1964) abound in Waters films; among them, the rat-on-Mrs.-Sterner's-shoe section in *Serial Mom* and the chicken execution and pigpen scenes in *Mondo Trasho*.

Douglas Sirk

Waters loves the opulent settings and garish colors of the films of this German-American director. Sirk's popular melodramas—"women's pictures" like *Magnificent Obsession* (1954) and *Written on the Wind* (1956)—offered a cynical vision of American postwar values, a vision Waters cranked up in each of his films. Lana Turner's friendship with her maid, Juanita Moore, in *Imitation of Life* (1959), a movie bursting with outsider and segregation motifs, is paralleled by that of Peggy Gravel and her maid Grizelda in *Desperate Living,* as are several other motifs and visuals from Sirk films.

Herschell Gordon Lewis

Once the undisputed king of horror movie gore, Lewis launched his grisly career in 1963 with the cult classic *Blood Feast.* The cheapjack fare that followed—*Monster a-Go Go* (1965), *A Taste of Blood* (1967), and *The Gore-Gore Girls* (1972)—played Baltimore drive-ins and helped shape Waters' taste for exploitation flicks. References to Lewis' films abound in Waters' stories. Posters and clips from Lewis' movies appear in *Serial Mom.*

Russ Meyer

The ultimate independent filmmaker, Meyer writes, produces, photographs, and distributes all of his films. His career autonomy, wild plots, and over-the-top characters were all early inspirations to Waters, who counts Meyer's *Faster, Pussycat! Kill! Kill!* (1965) among his all-time favorite films.

Kenneth Anger

This American independent filmmaker and author has impressed Waters on three levels: His original use of rock music in film; his hallmark film, *Scorpio Rising* (1963), a documentary on motorcyclists in New York City; and his books on Tinseltown scandal, *Hollywood Babylon* (1965) and *Hollywood Babylon II*

(1984). Waters attributes Anger's use of rock music in his films as inspiration for his own early rock-and-roll soundtracks. A direct reference to Anger occurs in *Mondo Trasho,* when Mary Vivian Pearce leafs through a copy of *Hollywood Babylon.*

Federico Fellini

The Italian director is among the most celebrated and distinctive post–World War II filmmakers. Like Waters' work, Fellini's distinctive, autobiographical films portray people at their most bizarre, and are marked by dreamlike or hallucinatory imagery on an otherwise ordinary situation. Waters' most Felliniesque moments include the depiction of the Crucifixion and the lobster-rape scene, both from *Multiple Maniacs.*

Jean Genet

This French criminal and social-outcast-turned-writer became a leading figure in the avant-garde theater of the '60s. While he was in film school, Waters rarely missed a performance of any Genet play, and he was also inspired by Genet's acclaimed first film, *Un Chant d'Amour.*

Ingmar Bergman

The Swedish film writer-director who achieved world fame with such movies as *The Seventh Seal* (1957) is noted for his versatile camera work and for his fragmented narrative style. But it's his bleak depiction of human vulnerability and despair that attracted Waters, and which is most evident as an influence on Waters' work.

Rainer Werner Fassbinder

This movie and theater director, writer, and actor was an important force in postwar West German cinema. Like Waters' movies, Fassbinder's socially conscious films often examine themes of oppression and despair.

Luis Buñuel

This Spanish director and filmmaker is known for his early surrealist films and his highly personal style. His films usually concern social injustice and, like Waters' films, often feature religious excesses.

Chapter Eleven
THE TRIUMPH OF HENNY PENNY

"MY FILMS AREN'T MEANT TO CHANGE ANYTHING, BUT IF THEY EVER DID, I'D BE HAPPY. MAYBE I'VE MADE TRASH ONE MILLIONTH MORE RESPECTABLE."

—John Waters

It's three days after the September 11, 2001, terrorist attacks on the United States, and nearly every television program in the nation is given over to coverage of the smoldering Pentagon and the collapsed World Trade Center towers. But the *Ricki Lake* show is concerned with a world crisis of another kind: white-trash teens whose mothers dress like sluts.

While Ricki's studio audience cheers, a fat, toothless hag in a sheer black peignoir and shiny go-go boots bumps and grinds her way onto the stage. She's a dead ringer for Edith Massey, but that comparison is probably lost on her teenage children, Frances and Christopher, who are explaining to Ricki that they want the kind of mom who bakes cookies, not the kind who works in a titty bar and hits on their school friends.

"My mom looks like a hooker, Ricki!" big-haired, tattooed Frances weeps. "When she takes me to school, she flashes her tits at people as we drive past!"

Mom grins and sticks out her tongue at the camera. "It's hot where we live! I'm just airin' 'em out!"

After Christopher complains that his mother is dating one of his classmates—"And one of the stupidest ones too!"—Ricki sends Mom offstage to be overhauled by the "Makeover Police." Mom returns later, looking like a frumpy dowager, and as she and her dazed children are led off the stage, Ricki reminds us that tomorrow her guests will be professional shoplifters and, on Friday, pregnant women who defiantly drink and drug.

Ricki Lake is living proof that John Waters has infiltrated the American middle class. Discovered by Waters while he was casting *Hairspray*, Lake is inarguably Waters' biggest star, having eclipsed even Divine's notoriety. Beloved by millions of middle-aged housewives, she went from unknown Dreamland hair hopper Tracy Turnblad to real-life trash talk-show maven. Her guests—septuagenarian titty dancers, transsexual lesbian prostitutes, corporate executives with diaper fetishes—are sleazeballs straight out of Mortville; the issues her show addresses—"Will Breast Implants Save Your Marriage?" "Which is Sexier, Fat or Skinny?"—are undeniably Watersian. Not long ago, Waters was vilified by critics for celebrating the underside of American culture; today, talk shows on every network make stars of these same wackos.

In the new millennium, John Waters—or at least the indisputable evidence of his impact on popular culture—is everywhere. On the radio, "Frontier Psychiatry," a song by U.K. band the Avalanches, features a sound sample from *Polyester*. On television, Mink Stole appears in a recurring role in MTV's cable soap *Spyder Games,* and her Think Mink column appears in dozens of newspapers across the country. A stage musical of *Hairspray*—reportedly starring Harvey Fierstein in the Divine roles—is being readied for Broadway.

On street corners from Phoenix to Westport, Ricki Lake smiles down from mammoth four-color billboards promoting her talk show. On the side of a building on San Francisco's Lyon Street, a graffiti artist has spray-painted EDITH MASSEY in large, black letters; on the wall of a church on Divisadero Street, another artist responds with MONA MONTGOMERY! In the 1960s, Waters was more likely to be found in court battling censorship than on *Lifestyles of the Rich and Famous,* on which he appeared in the 1990s.

"Boy, was I a ham bone!" he says of his *Lifestyles* appearance. "I never thought that they would run it. Because I would point to stuff in my house and say things like 'I found this in the trash,' 'This cost a nickel,' or 'I stole it.'"

If scandal, sleaze, and celebrity worship have become our national religion, then John Waters is an American prophet. For more than 30 years, this Baltimore-based sage has been joyfully asserting—in his movies, writings, and talk show guest shots—that freedom is just another word for the right to love tabloid television. Waters was a murder trial buff whose fascination with criminal justice predated Court TV; an aficionado of serial killers long before it became fashionable; a fan of camp and kitsch before these words had entered the lexicon.

The little boy who wished the sky had fallen has infiltrated the dreary workaday world with his glamorous vision of trash. He's been lampooned, cast in leads, even copied; critics who dismissed him as "underground" write today of his influence and refer to Waters as a "star maker."

But you won't find Waters taking credit for anyone's celebrity. When he's praised for discovering a star or kick-starting a career, he displays his usual largesse: "They're certainly not 'my' people. They're my *peers*. Ricki Lake did it on her own. Pat Moran won the Emmy for casting (network television drama) *Homicide*. Vince Peranio is the production designer on that show. Baltimore is like one big showbiz town. It's great. But it's not because I became famous and everyone flocked here."

Maybe not. But there's no denying the impact that John Waters' curious vision has had on popular culture. The success of his teen-angst comedies *Hairspray* and *Cry-Baby* signaled his arrival in the mainstream, and where coverage of his films had once been consigned to the pages of underground screen 'zines, he was suddenly being covered by *Time* and writing guest commentaries for *Newsweek*. By the 1990s the world had morphed into a bizarrely Watersian place, filled with scary, captivating people: Jeffrey Dahmer was an *über*-celebrity; Joey Buttafuoco was a white-trash hero; and Lorena Bobbitt became famous for cutting off her husband's penis and tossing it into an empty field.

The Menendez brothers could easily be John Waters characters: sexy, stupid rich kids who killed their parents because their father forced them to give him blow jobs. Tonya Harding is a misguided Mortvillian—Princess Coo-Coo on skates, if you will—her pipe-toting henchmen straight out of Queen Carlotta's castle. At the end of the 20th century, Connie and Raymond Marble had nothing on Marv Albert, O.J. Simpson, or even uptight Brit Hugh Grant.

In John Waters' peculiar take on the world, the filthiest people alive were demented but fictional. Twenty years later, they were acting out a reality not even Waters could have envisioned: the president of the United States, his dim-witted bimbo, and her flabby, horse-faced gal pal, all discussing a semen-stained cocktail dress on national television. Who needs Connie Marble when you've got Linda Tripp tapping phones and *The New York Times* reporting that the president of the United States inserted his cigar into an intern's vagina? As the century drew to a close, Bill Clinton was playing the Divine role in a real-life Watersian comedy, and the sight of the president eating shit may have been enough to make even Waters himself gag.

Today, John Waters is respectable. The mayor of Baltimore declared February 7, 1985 "John Waters Day," and the Independent Film Channel tapped him as the host of its Independent Sprit Awards. His films are even the subject of a class at the University of Iowa.

"I never thought *that* would happen," Waters says. "I'm flattered. I never went to film school, but I don't think my movies are bad for students. They cost $5,000 and they're still playing, so I guess I did something right."

Waters' most successful film, *Hairspray,* of course, cost substantially more. The story originated with an article Waters wrote for *Baltimore Magazine* in 1985 about that city's legendary *Buddy Deane Show,* a teen dance program patterned on Philadelphia's *American Bandstand.* The show ran from 1957 to 1964 and was among Waters' earliest obsessions. *Hairspray* is about *The Corny Collins Show*—a spoof of *Buddy Deane*—and race relations in 1960s Baltimore.

The director wanted infamous sex-change patient Christine Jorgensen to play Edna Turnblad, the mother of teen hair hopper Tracy, who he wanted to be played by Divine. But New Line, which bankrolled the film's $3 million budget, balked at the oddball casting. The company was hesitant to green-light a movie in which an obese 40-year-old drag queen was seen making out with teenage boys. New Line didn't want Divine involved in the picture at all, but Waters compromised: He rewrote the part of Tracy's mother, Edna, for Divine, and the film went into preproduction with the working title *White Lipstick.*

Waters assembled the surviving Dreamlanders and rounded out the cast with some of his favorite has-beens and *über*-stars, most notably Pia Zadora. He hired Debbie Harry, Sonny Bono, Ruth Brown, and Ric Ocasek—a cast *The Baltimore Sun* described as "a selection of used-up former celebrities whose failed careers are part of the joke."

"I don't think of them as has-beens, that's a mean term," says Waters. "To me, they're true originals."

He recalls that Bono was worried about the script. "He kept saying, 'Everything that's in the move is in this script, right?' Like I was going to add a shit-eating scene or something as soon as Sonny's back was turned."

Waters cast Ricki Lake, a college student and would-be actor, in her first film role as 15-year-old Tracy Turnblad. Lake was the first of a new generation of Dreamlanders, a jovial, middle-class Baltimorean who aspired to trashiness and brought something new to a Waters film: cheerfulness.

Because the film deals with race relations, it's ironic that Jean Hill, the only black Dreamlander, isn't in it. Waters remembers, "She broke her leg a month before we started shooting. I tried every possible way to get her in it, right up to the last minute. I even talked to her doctor, and he said she wouldn't be able to walk." Unable to convince the insurance company to cover Hill, a disappointed Waters moved on without her.

Surprisingly, *Hairspray*'s politics went largely unnoticed by critics, who almost unanimously praised the film. Audiences also loved *Hairspray*. Though the movie's characters and situations were comparatively tame for a John Waters picture, they were shocking in a suburban shopping mall theater. Moviegoers who discovered John Waters with *Hairspray* weren't seeing him through the prism of his earlier, more unusual films; for first-time Waters audiences, the sight of a fat man playing Jerry Stiller's wife in a movie about a teenage dance show was just plain weird.

Hairspray received its first public screening at the Miami Film

Festival. Divine took his mother, with whom he'd recently reconciled after a long separation. Mrs. Milstead was happy to have her son back and—once the shock of having a famous drag queen for a son wore off—delighted with the turn his career had taken.

"It was a good time for Glenny," she remembers. "He was really famous, which was what he always wanted, and he was getting a lot more work, and that always made him happy."

The good time didn't last. The week after *Hairspray* opened to rave reviews, Divine—who'd battled ill health for years—died of a heart attack in Los Angeles. He was there to make an appearance on Fox's *Married...With Children* in what he hoped would become a recurring role. Divine died the night before shooting began.

Waters was devastated.

"They'll never say it to my face," he told *Melody Maker* in 1988, "but a lot of studio execs will be relieved that the next time I have a project, they won't have to deal with the Divine issue. Even after all these years, he scared them."

Hairspray's success signaled the second phase of Waters' career, one that would find him making bigger-budget Hollywood films. He became, with the commercial and critical success of *Hairspray,* a hot Hollywood commodity. For the first time, he didn't have to look for a backer for his next picture.

Cry-Baby was Water's first studio film, released by Universal in 1990 and produced by Ron Howard's Imagine Entertainment. It was also Waters' first out-and-out musical. The movie's $10 million budget was modest by Hollywood standards but a fortune for a Waters film. He had, for the first time, genuine stars on the roster: Johnny Depp, fresh from his success on television's *21 Jump Street,* was an A-List actor, and Polly Bergen was a still-respectable "Old Hollywood" name. In support of these notable leads was the usual group of has-beens (David Nelson, Troy Donahue, and Joey Heatherton), fringe stars (punker Iggy Pop, porn queen Traci Lords, and infamous newspaper heiress and Symbionese Liberation Army abductee Patricia Hearst), and, of course, Dreamlanders—although the latter, with the exception of newcomer Ricki Lake, are barely in evidence in the finished film.

While he delighted in the perks of a big-budget picture—"I never thought I would ever see the day when I would see Hollywood billboards for one of my films!"—wags wondered if Waters hadn't sold out in making a commercial movie.

Waters didn't care. "I've always wanted to sell out," he quipped to every reporter he met at the time. "The problem is, nobody wanted to buy me."

He defended Hollywood and claimed to have enjoyed working in the studio system. "It was very positive for me; I liked it. And the people were, in some ways, less difficult than some of the people I had to deal with in the past. The hardest part was getting them to agree to make the movie in the first place."

The idea for *Cry-Baby* came from a Baltimore murder case that Waters remembered from his childhood. "A Drapette had been murdered," he recalls, "and the nuns were all saying, 'See what happens when you're *bad*?'"

Cry-Baby, a spoof of rock-and-roll juvenile delinquent films of the '50s, is an anti-Cinderella story about a good girl, Allison Vernon-Williams (Amy Locane), who wants to be bad. She pursues Baltimore's most notorious hood, Cry-Baby (Depp), and sings a number of once-popular rock tunes along the way. Eventually, true love triumphs, and after a chicken race and a lot of good-versus-bad setups, the two ride off into the Baltimore sunset.

Like the story that inspired it, many of the film's situations and locales were culled from Waters' life. "The charm school was very much like the cotillion I had to go to as a kid, with dancing class and that kind of crap." Mrs. Vernon-Williams' speech about the "Four B's" (beauty, brains, breeding, bounty) is one that Waters' grandmother, Stella Whitaker, used to recite to him when he was a child.

Once it was finished, *Cry-Baby* received the widest release of any Waters picture to date, playing in nearly 1,500 theaters. (*Hairspray* had been booked into only about 200 movie houses.) When *Cry-Baby* was screened at the Cannes Film Festival in 1990, the film and its maker were greeted with a standing ovation. But the film received a very different reception from audiences elsewhere.

"On opening night, when I walked into the Waverly Theater and there were two empty seats, I knew it was not going to work," Waters remembers.

The film's wider distribution was partly to blame for its lukewarm reception. *Cry-Baby* played to suburban audiences in tiny, one-theater towns whose audiences had never seen a John Waters film. Without the reference point of his previous movies, mainstream audiences thought the film was odd.

Waters contends that the movie failed in the United States because it spoofed genres of film that its young audience wasn't familiar with. The folks who knew the Elvis musicals and JD flicks that *Cry-Baby* spoofed weren't going to John Waters films in 1990. The film's younger audiences, Waters believes, didn't get the jokes.

"A teenage girl flying through the air and landing in her lover's arms is only funny if you've seen a couple of beach party movies or one of the Ann-Margret–Elvis musicals," Waters says. "In Paris they revere that kind of American juvenile delinquent movie."

That may explain *Cry-Baby*'s success in Europe, where it scored a bigger box office than any previous Waters film. It was especially popular in Australia and France, where it got rave reviews.

Stateside, Waters' hard-core fans felt differently about his new movie. They complained that its heroes were too normal for a Waters film. Without Divine as an anchor, with Dreamlanders reduced to cameos, and with filth once more taking a backseat to nostalgia, *Cry-Baby* didn't wash with Waters' camp followers. Critics made much of this point, several of them pining for the days when a John Waters film guaranteed a certain shock value.

"That was really annoying," Waters says. "The critics who said they wished *Cry-Baby* were more like *Pink Flamingos* were the same critics who hated *Pink Flamingos* when it first came out."

Regardless of what critics wrote about him, John Waters was by now a household name. After *Cry-Baby* his Hollywood clout continued to grow, and his films featured even bigger stars—Kathleen Turner, Melanie Griffith—and reached wider audiences than ever before.

1994's *Serial Mom,* starring Turner and featuring Mink Stole, was the antithesis of his last two pictures. Where *Hairspray* and *Cry-Baby,* both musicals, were arguably "family" films, *Serial Mom* took broad swipes at the genre and spoofed the very idea of the nuclear family with its story of the Sutphins, a wholesome sit-com clan whose mother is a serial killer.

The transition between Dreamland old and new is played out on the screen in *Serial Mom*'s uproarious courtroom battles between movie star Turner and former Waters star Mink Stole. Where Stole was once the featured performer, here she's a supporting player to Turner's star turn.

Still, Stole enjoyed the role. "Kathleen Turner was a long-established movie star by the time I met her," Stole says, "and to be able to call her 'pig fucker,' that's something to be proud of. Not many can lay claim to something like that."

After *Serial Mom,* which received mixed reviews but proved popular with fans, Waters returned to more autobiographical fare. Both *Pecker* (1998) and *Cecil B. Demented* (2000) were greeted by fans and critics as romans à clef. *Pecker* is the story of a light-hearted photographer whose wacky friends and family pose for his voyeuristic photos; when Pecker is unexpectedly embraced by the New York art world and lauded by the mainstream press, he has to learn to balance his fame without surrendering his obsessions. *Cecil* concerns a guerrilla filmmaker who makes no-budget films and lives in squalor in downtown Baltimore.

"*Pecker* reflects two sides of my life that I'm very fond of: blue-collar Baltimore and the New York art world," Waters says. "Every weekend, I have to decide if I want to go to a biker luau or a dinner after an opening at the Museum of Modern Art."

Waters' favorite review for the film came from *The Japan Times,* which called *Pecker* "a Disney film for perverts." American critics, on the other hand, devoted more column inches to the film's title than to its premise.

"I liked the name *Pecker* because writing it and saying it out loud made me laugh," Waters says. "And I thought that I could get away with using it, which I did, but only barely. The Motion Picture Association of America first said we couldn't use that name, but we got it overturned. The foreign translation is tricky, though. It should be *Willie* in England, but then my explanation for his nickname doesn't work—the idea that his family calls him that because he pecks at his food. Because there's nothing especially sexual about peckers in the movie. Like everything else about Pecker's family, in context it's completely normal. Out of context, people snigger and laugh. Irony changes everything."

Pecker is almost entirely concerned with the curtain of irony between blue-collar Baltimore and the New York art world, and Pecker's subjects are among Waters' own: lesbian strippers, teenage hair hoppers, roach-infested fast food, copulating rats, and the whacked-out weirdos of downtown Bumberg.

"*Pecker* has some of the edge of my earlier movies, but a sweeter spirit," Waters said at the time. "The sense of humor is the same. *Pecker* is a feel-good movie for lunatics."

Waters demurred when journalists asked if *Pecker* was autobiographical. "It's a fair question, but I'm not Pecker. The difference is that I was in on the irony of my career from the beginning. I was ambitious. I read *Variety* from the time I was 12 years old. I was very anxious for someone from New York to discover me, and it didn't happen accidentally. I tried for eight years to show my films in New York."

To some degree, *Pecker* is a reflection of Waters' recent reinvention as a gallery artist. His photographic pieces, which he calls "redirecting jobs," are serial images culled from various movies (his own and others') that Waters assembles into thematic or chronological framed pieces. These conceptual and often comedic assemblages have shown in galleries around the country and have been collected in a coffee table book titled *Director's Cut*.

Pecker concludes by announcing "the end of irony," but Waters was never more ironic than in the comic condemnation of Hollywood filmmaking that would eventually become *Cecil B. Demented*. Waters actually began work on *Cecil* shortly after *Serial Mom*'s release in 1994, but when the project—which was then about a Hollywood movie star who comes to Baltimore and falls in love with a truck driver—wasn't well received, Waters began work on *Pecker*.

(Waters had had similar luck with *Glamourpuss,* a film that Paramount picked up for development shortly after *Cry-Baby*'s release in 1990. The screenplay told the story of a white boy who wants to be black and who fights off a skinhead invasion of his hometown with the help of a friendly fag hag. "I pitched it as *Mahogany* meets *The Battle of Algiers*," Waters recalls. "And the studio laughed right in my face." Paramount put the picture into turnaround and Waters moved on to *Serial Mom*.)

By the time Canal Plus films bankrolled *Cecil B. Demented,* Waters had rewritten the script. In the new version, Cecil (Stephen Dorff) was a struggling Baltimore "guerrilla filmmaker" who kidnaps a big movie star (Melanie Griffith) and forces her to be in his film *Raving Beauty* as a political statement against the big-budget Hollywood productions he despises.

"It's my action epic—*Die Hard* for the Hollywood-impaired," Waters said of the film, which also starred Alicia Witt (of television's *Cybill*). *Cecil* featured the usual Dreamlander bits from Mink Stole, Mary Vivian Pearce, Ricki Lake, and Patty Hearst, who, in a typical Waters spoof, played the mother of a terrorist kidnapper.

Cecil was, as Waters himself said, "the craziest film I've done in years." (The film's title originated in a review Waters received early in his career in which a film critic referred to him as "Cecil B. Demented.") Despite its tiny-by-Hollywood-standards $10 million budget and bizarre characters and situations, Waters' oldest fans once again complained that he'd sold out—an especially ironic charge, considering the film's anti-Hollywood posturing. Internet postings on several Waters fan sites whined about Mink Stole's tiny role and about Waters working once again with a big-name star like Griffith—who expertly spoofed her own image in the film.

"Melanie got magazine covers that I could never get, like *Ladies' Home Journal*," Waters said. "I mean, she got my picture in *Parade*! I've always wanted to be in *Parade*!"

The director was unmoved by the criticism. "First I made underground movies, and then there were no underground movies. Then it was midnight movies, and they disappeared. Then independent movies, but they were co-opted by Hollywood. Now it's all the same. So I make Hollywood movies."

In true Waters fashion, he was already pitching his next film during the press junket for *Cecil B. Demented*. "I haven't done a sex movie in a while," he told reporters. "My next one is about sex addicts in a blue-collar neighborhood, and their struggle for dignity. It's called *A Dirty Shame*, which is an expression I love." Then he added, "Remember when sex addicts used to be just called *horny*?"

Waters also acknowledged that while times may have changed, the opinions of some mainstream critics haven't. "There are people who still hate my films," he says. "That's OK. I still get offended at a lot of films, too. Look, I was offended by *Forrest Gump*. When Forrest Gump started to run, it offended my community standards. What toll-free number do I call when *my* community is offended?"

Ironically, as the world becomes trashier and Waters' films become sweeter, his reputation as the King of Trash looms larger.

Waters' art has taken a backseat to his legend, and as the long-time arbiter of all things tasteless, he's left happily holding the blame for all that's sleazy in pop culture today.

"I was always criticized for bad taste," Waters gleefully admits. "It wasn't bad taste. It was *my* taste. And now it's cool to be trashy.

"My humor and American humor have moved amazingly closer to one another. Who knows, *Pink Flamingos* may someday play on television. Anything can happen. Today mainstream movies like *There's Something About Mary* have close-ups of come and testicles caught in zippers. I think that's great. It makes my life easier when movies like that are out there and make money and are big hits. That would have been unheard of 10 years ago, and I like to think I've had a little bit of influence in making that possible. I'm proud of that."

Waters' influence has reached beyond just film. Divine made RuPaul possible; he paved the way for cross-dressing runway models and even two-dimensional, gender-confused line drawings. When Walt Disney's big-screen animated feature *The Little Mermaid* (1989) featured a flamboyant squid named Ursula (voiced by gruff-voiced television actress Pat Carroll), the more-than-passing resemblance to Divine wasn't lost on a single critic.

Characters based on Waters himself have also turned up in a pair of animated television programs: Warner Bros.' *Toonsylvania* features a character named Dr. Vic who's a dead ringer for Waters, and the villainous, pencil-mustached Mr. Fish on MTV's *Spy Groove* is clearly a send-up of the director. Waters even appeared as himself on a 1997 episode of *The Simpsons,* titled "Homer's Phobia," in which Waters plays the openly gay owner of Cockamamies, a zany collectibles shop.

"I was so happy," he says of his *Simpsons* appearance. "It was my goal to be a cartoon character since I was 5 years old. The only thing that surprised me about the script, since you record your voice partway before they animate it, was that I actually danced with Bart Simpson on the show."

The vision of the King of Trash waltzing with Bart Simpson secured Waters' place in pop culture once and for all. Once known only as an underground filmmaker, Waters is today an icon, a symbol of our preoccupation with all things cheap and tacky. Whether appearing as himself in documentaries about filmmaking (*Anthem*, 1997) or TV tributes to his friends (VH1's *Behind the Music: Blondie*) or as an actor in films by other famous directors (Jonathan Demme's *Something Wild*, 1986; Woody Allen's *Sweet and Lowdown*, 1999), Waters is always enormously trashy. He is always the little boy from Baltimore who wished the sky would fall. Perhaps his greatest achievement is that he's brought the heavens crashing down on all of us, and we're just as delighted about it as he is.

"These days, I'm petrified I'll die in a car accident," Waters says about the little boy who searched the city dump looking for smashed autos all those years ago. "But even if I do, I'll have had a really good life. Because life is nothing if you're not obsessed."

FILMOGRAPHY

HAG IN A BLACK LEATHER JACKET

1964, 8mm black and white, 17 minutes

Starring Mary Vivian Pearce and Mona Montgomery

Written, directed, produced, and photographed by John Waters

SYNOPSIS: This surreal short film depicts the wedding of a white woman (Mona Montgomery) to a black man. He arrives at her home with a garbage can in the front seat of his car. She leaves with him. Later she dresses in a ballerina costume and dances for him. Then her intended climbs into the garbage can, and she loads the can into his car.

The couple and their friends convene on a rooftop. Mona is wearing a bridal gown; the wedding guests are dressed in costumes made from tinfoil and American flags. The black man climbs out of his garbage can, and the guests (who include a child and a man in a dress) eat wedding cake. A Ku Klux Klansman descends from the roof's chimney and marries the couple.

Mary Vivian Pearce dances the Bodie Green. The final image is of a piece of paper with "The End" written on it being flushed down a toilet.

TRIVIA: The film was shot around and on top of Waters' parents' home. Pearce is wearing a cocktail dress "borrowed" from Waters' mother, who provided the piano accompaniment heard on the film's soundtrack.

ROMAN CANDLES

1966, three 8mm color reels shown simultaneously, 40 minutes

Starring Maelcum Soul, Bob Skidmore, Mona Montgomery, Divine, Mink Stole, Mary Vivian Pearce, and David Lochary

Written, directed, produced, and photographed by John Waters

SYNOPSIS: *Roman Candles* contains random scenes of Waters' friends simulating depraved acts: A junkie is seen shooting heroin; a fashion model rides a motorcycle; Mink Stole sobs at a graveside; a 300-pound fag hag named Alexis eats an entire bowl of fruit. Maelcum Soul, dressed as a nun, drinks beer and makes out with her boyfriend, Dudley, who is dressed as a priest. Mona Montgomery, in a bridal gown, simulates sex with Bob Skidmore and Mark Isherwood, while Pat Moran performs to Nancy Sinatra's "These Boots Were Made for Walkin'" and later spanks Mink Stole, who's wearing a silver miniskirt. David Lochary reads *The Wizard of Oz* to Maelcum, who throws fits while Bob attacks Mary Vivian Pearce with an electric fan. Finally, Maelcum takes off all her clothes and later plays hide-and-seek with Divine.

TRIVIA: This was the first film to be shot at Dreamland Studios, which was actually Waters' bedroom in his parents' house.

EAT YOUR MAKEUP

1968, 16mm black and white, 45 minutes

Starring Maelcum Soul, David Lochary, Marina Melin, Divine, Mary Vivian Pearce, and Mona Montgomery

Written, directed, produced, and photographed by John Waters

SYNOPSIS: *Eat Your Makeup* tells the story of a governess (Soul) and her boyfriend (Lochary) who kidnap models (Melin, Pearce, and Montgomery) and force them to model themselves to death in front of an audience. The women are given only eyeliner and mascara to eat.

In a fantasy sequence, the assassination of John F. Kennedy is recreated, with Divine as Jackie Kennedy and Howard Gruber as JFK.

TRIVIA: The film was shot mostly on the front lawn of Waters' parents' home and at various Baltimore locations. Waters, inspired by the famous Zapruder film, created a JFK sequence that predates Oliver Stone's similar homage by more than 20 years. Dreamland star Maelcum Soul died shortly after this film's premiere.

MONDO TRASHO

1969, 16mm black-and-white, 93 minutes

A Dreamland Production

Starring Mary Vivian Pearce, Divine, David Lochary, and Mink Stole. With Bob Skidmore, Margie Skidmore, Berenica Cipcus, Jack Walsh, Chris Atkinson, Lizzy Temple Black, Mark Isherwood, Mike Bauer, Pat Moran, George Figgs, Susan Lowe, George Tamsitt, Marina Melin, Sharon Sandrock, Gilbert McGill, Tricia Waters, Alan Reese, Rick Morrow, and Mimi Lochary. And introducing John Leisenring as "The Shrimper."

Production assistance: David Lochary, Bob Skidmore

Produced, directed, written, filmed, and edited by John Waters

SYNOPSIS: Bonnie (Mary Vivian Pearce) is having a bad day. After visiting the park, where she feeds ground round to cockroaches and has a sexual encounter with a pervert (John Leisenring), she gets run over by Lady Divine (Divine), who's driving a 1959 Cadillac Eldorado. Divine takes the unconscious Bonnie to a Laundromat, where the Virgin Mother of God appears, accompanied by an angel (Lizzy Temple Black).

Later, Mink Stole, Divine, and Bonnie are tossed into a local loony bin, where Mink does a topless tap-dance routine and then gets raped by the inmates. Divine hijacks a taxicab to the office of Dr. Coat Hanger (David Lochary), who amputates Bonnie's feet and grafts on a pair of monster feet in their place. After a

shoot-out with the police, Divine and Bonnie stumble into a pigpen, where Divine dies. Bonnie clicks her new feet together and
is magically transported to a busy Baltimore street, where a hill-
billy moons her from his car. She clicks her feet together again
and is transported to another street, where two women (Mink
Stole, Mimi Lochary) whisper nasty things about her—"Maybe
she's a draft dodger…a jet-setter…a dinge queen…a peacenik…"
Finally, Bonnie clicks her heels together again and vanishes.

BEST MOMENTS: The Virgin Mother of God appears to Divine
in a Laundromat; Divine pulls a knife on a bored taxi driver.

LOW POINT: Over the main credits, a man in executioner's garb
beheads chickens, which flop around in mud puddles.

BEST DIALOGUE:
Divine: Oh, Mary! Oh, Mary! Oh, God, oh, Holy Trinity! Oh,
Mary! Oh, Mary! Oh, Mary! Oh, Mary!

Divine: It isn't easy being Divine. Oh, the Good Lord knows that
it is not, for he has blessed me and at the same time has caused
me to trouble through Original Sin. I am but merely Divine.

Divine: I can only pray so hard!

WHAT TO WATCH FOR: Divine continually hiking up her capri
pants throughout the picture; the old lady in the thrift store who
watches Divine shoplift; in the foot-amputation scene, Dr. Coat
Hanger knocks his nurse's cap off, but it pops back on in the next
shot, then disappears again while the nurse is vomiting.

WATERSISMS: Auto-related death, vomit, abortion, animal sex,
shoplifting, capital punishment, car fetishism, foot fetishism,
garbage, nature, mental hospitals, the Virgin Mary, a staircase.

DREAMLANDER ALERT: David Lochary and Mink Stole do double duty: He as Dr. Hanger and also one of the nuthouse inmates; she as the topless tap dancer and one of the two women at the end of the story. David Lochary's mother, Mimi, plays the other woman, and her son provides her voice-over. Pat Moran is Dr. Hanger's receptionist. John Waters' sister, Tricia, is the girl Dr. Hanger tries to pick up, and Waters himself appears, in voice-over, as a tabloid reporter.

READING MATERIAL ALERT: On the bus, Bonnie reads *Hollywood Babylon* by Kenneth Anger. Also, Dr. Hanger's snotty receptionist reads *The Image*.

PRETENTIOUS THEORY ABOUT THIS FILM: *Mondo Trasho's* melancholy tone can be attributed to its soundtrack. Naïve pop songs create an unattainable fantasy of love.

Waters also employs pseudoreligious pop songs that use the terminology of religion and insanity to describe the state of being in love. Insanity-themed love songs, which Waters uses during scenes of psychotic breakdowns in the film, also help set the tone.

TRIVIA: Most of the cast was arrested on "indecent exposure" charges during filming of the hitchhiker sequence. In the final scene, one of the women refers to a "hair hopper," a term that would be used again in *Hairspray*. Some of the songs in *Mondo Trasho* would also be used in later Waters productions. Not counting the full-length, rarely seen version of *Female Trouble,* which is 95 minutes long, this is Waters' longest feature film at 93 minutes.

WHAT THE CRITICS SAID:
The 300-pound sex symbol, Divine, is undoubtedly some sort of discovery.

—*Los Angeles Free Press*

A very amusing satire on films that exploit sex, violence, and seaminess. Should give pause to some established filmmakers who think they have their fingers on the pulse of the film-going public.

—Variety

There is a gap here all right, a sensitivity gap, and those that laugh are in more trouble than they know.

—The Baltimore Sun

An underground epic of all that is trashy in life.

—Provincetown Advocate

An insane, fabulous adventure story.

—Show

Waters' longest film, and you can feel every minute of it.

—Video Movie Guide

THE DIANE LINKLETTER STORY

1969, 16mm black and white, 15 minutes

Starring David Lochary, Mary Vivian Pearce, and Divine

Written, directed, produced, and photographed by John Waters

SYNOPSIS: A dramatization of the tragic suicide of Art Linkletter's daughter, Diane, this short experimental film was made primarily to test Waters' new sound camera. In it, Pearce and Lochary improvise dialogue about their delinquent daughter, Diane, played by Divine. Diane comes home while her parents are talking about her drug use and miscreant behavior. The three quarrel, and Diane goes upstairs and leaps from her bedroom window.

BEST MOMENT: Over the opening credits, Divine (as Diane) joyously does drugs.

LOW POINT: Mary Vivian Pearce and David Lochary ad-lib dialogue while they wait for Divine's entrance.

BEST DIALOGUE:
Diane: I love Jim. He's a groovy guy. He's got a groovy short.
Dad: What are you talking like this for?
Mom: Short?
Diane: Car! Car!

WHAT TO WATCH FOR: Diane's 5 o'clock shadow.

WATERSISMS: Drugs, juvenile delinquency, fame.

TRIVIA: This story is a highly fictionalized account of Art Linkletter's daughter Diane's suicide and was filmed entirely on October 5, 1969, the day after she jumped out the window of her sixth-floor apartment at 8787 Shoreham Dr. in West Hollywood, Calif. Diane Linkletter was 20 years old at the time of her death. The film's soundtrack spoofs on "Dear Mom and Dad" and "We Love You, Call Collect," a record by Art and Diane Linkletter. The film was shot in Waters' apartment; note the Warhol portrait of Liz Taylor in the background.

The film was never released commercially, though it did play the college circuit for a short time. *The Diane Linkletter Story* has surfaced as a bootleg videocassette, usually paired with a recording of Divine's stage play *The Neon Woman*.

MULTIPLE MANIACS

1970, 16mm black and white, 90 minutes

A Dreamland Production

Starring Divine, David Lochary, Mary Vivian Pearce, Mink Stole. With Cookie Mueller, Edith Massey, Susan Lowe, Rick Morrow, Howard Gruber, Paul Swift, Vince Peranio, Jim Thompson, Dee Vitolo, Ed Peranio, Bob Skidmore, Margie Skidmore, Jack Walsh, Susan Walsh, Gilbert McGill, Pat Moran, Paul Landis, Mark Lazarus, Harvey Fred, Suzie Nichols, Steve Waters, Julia Richardson, Will Cullen, Jack Roberts, Mark Isherwood, Berenica Cipcus, Hawley Peterson, Tom Wells, Michael Renner Jr., and Cowboy. And George Figgs as Jesus Christ.

Stills: Lawrence Irving
Production assistance: David Lochary, Howard Gruber, Bob Skidmore, Jack Walsh, Mink Stole
Lobstora by Vince Peranio

Produced, directed, written, filmed, and edited by John Waters

SYNOPSIS: Inside a small circus tent in suburban Baltimore, Lady Divine's Cavalcade of Perversions performs: A woman licks a bicycle seat; two men lick a woman's armpits; two queers kiss each other; a man shoots up heroin; a group of naked people form a pyramid; the Puke Eater vomits into a bucket and then scoops it back into his mouth. After the show, Lady Divine (Divine) and her thugs steal their audience's money, jewels, and narcotics.

Divine has convinced Mr. David (David Lochary), who is having an affair with Bonnie (Mary Vivian Pearce), that he murdered Sharon Tate. David and Bonnie meet at a bar called Pete's, where barmaid Edith (Edith Massey) calls Divine to tell her that her boyfriend is sneaking around on her. On her way to confront Mr. David, Divine is raped by a hippie chick and a bearded transvestite from the Cavalcade. The Infant of Prague (Michael Renner Jr.) appears and takes Divine to a church, where she undergoes a religious conversion and reflects on the various miracles performed by Jesus. She meets a beautiful woman named Mink (Mink Stole), a religious whore who performs a "rosary job" on Divine ("And all at once, she inserted her rosary into one of my most private parts!") while reciting the stations of the cross. Divine fantasizes about the Crucifixion of Christ. Afterward, Mink and Divine murder a police officer.

David and Bonnie plan to kill Divine, who lives with her daughter, Cookie (Cookie Mueller). At Cookie's apartment, Bonnie accidentally shoots and kills Cookie, and David reads in the paper that Charles Manson killed Sharon Tate and realizes that Divine has lied to him about his involvement in the crime. Divine and Mink arrive, and Divine stabs Bonnie and David to death. She removes David's heart and eats it.

Divine discovers Cookie's body and goes berserk. Lobstora, a giant boiled lobster, arrives and rapes Divine, who heads for downtown Baltimore, where she's cornered and gunned down by the National Guard.

BEST MOMENT: The Infant of Prague appears to Divine.

LOW POINTS: Divine and Mink make out; a man injects heroin on a church altar.

BEST DIALOGUE:
Mr. David to Bonnie: Honey, have you ever killed anyone before?
Bonnie: No, but it would be something new.

Mr. David [*on being accused of homosexuality*]: Even Liberace would be more appealing to anyone with the particular neurosis you so rudely attribute to me.

Mink Stole [*complaining about the peculiar problems of being a religious whore*]: And Lent, shit, forget it! I gotta hang in synagogues then, and it's just not the same thing.

Bonnie to Mr. David: Nobody has been near my private parts except for this old lady I met on the bus.

WHAT TO WATCH FOR: Divine's naked ass; a delightful performance by Michael Renner Jr. as the Infant of Prague; Jesus feeding the multitudes with canned tuna and Wonder Bread; decorations in Cookie's apartment such as posters from *Night Games; I, a Woman; I, a Woman 2; Vixen,* and *Boom!*; a silk screen of Warhol's Jackie Kennedy portrait; a framed photo of the late Maelcum Soul that's visible in one scene; when Lobstora rapes Divine, the feet of Vincent Peranio and his brother (who are inside the Lobstora costume); suburban houses in the background during Christ's torture and death; and, in the "rosary job" scene, Mink Stole touching each church pew as she heads toward Divine—a necessity since, without her glasses, Stole was practically blind and could find her "mark" only by counting pews.

WATERSISMS: Vomit, Catholicism, the Virgin Mary, fame, drugs, staircases.

DREAMLANDER ALERT: Mink Stole, Cookie Mueller, and Mary Vivian Pearce do double duty as audience members in the Cavalcade of Perversion scene (Pat Moran is there too); Mink is also one of the women of Jerusalem in the eighth station of the cross; Edie plays both herself and the Virgin Mary; the guy in the car that Divine destroys is Steve Waters, John's brother.

PRETENTIOUS THEORY ABOUT THIS FILM: With the Cavalcade of Perversions, Waters is representing his relationship to his own audience, as well as the relationship between performers/exhibitionists and audience members/voyeurs in general. The Cavalcade is a metaphor for Dreamland Productions itself, and Mr. David represents Waters. Dreamland and the Cavalcade are both freak shows, in a sense, appealing to the audience's base instincts and curiosity. Mr. David lures customers into the show by telling them how sickening it is; Waters used similar claims in hyping his own early movies. His audience knows they'll be shocked and horrified, and yet they—like the suburban voyeurs who come to the Cavalcade—willingly pay to see his films. They feel compelled to watch, just as the lowlifes in the Cavalcade feel compelled to perform. This is the basis, really, for all entertainment: The sick symbiosis of voyeurs and exhibitionists. The freak show is just an extreme example.

TRIVIA: The title is an homage to Herschell Gordon Lewis' *Two Thousand Maniacs!* (1964), probably his best-known film. Lobstora was inspired by a postcard Waters often saw in Provincetown, depicting a beach with a giant lobster superimposed in the sky above it.

WHAT THE CRITICS SAID:
Not only uglier and more repulsive than *Mondo Trasho*, it is even more repugnant than *The Conqueror Worm*. Waters' first talkie is also his first sickie. As usual, the audience laughed most when Waters was at his sickest. [The audience seems] most appreciative when blood is being spilled and knives are being plunged. Is this part of the New World they have in mind?
—*The Baltimore Evening Sun*

Divine is incredible! She could start a whole new trend in films.
—KSFX, San Francisco

filthy

You have never, and I mean never, seen any movie remotely like *Multiple Maniacs*. Its jet-black humor goes beyond anything ever put on film. It is skillfully made, devastating in its black humor, low down and raunchy and frighteningly relevant to today—can only be compared to Tod Browning's *Freaks*.

—*Los Angeles Free Press*

PINK FLAMINGOS

1972, 16mm color, 93 minutes

A Fine Line Features/Dreamland Studios production

Starring Divine, David Lochary, Mary Vivian Pearce, Mink Stole, and introducing Danny Mills. With Edith Massey, Channing Wilroy, Cookie Mueller, Paul Swift, Susan Walsh, Linda Olgeirson, Pat Moran, Jack Walsh, Bob Skidmore, Pat LeFalver, Jackie Sidel, Julie Manschauer, Steve Yeager, Nancy Crystal, George Figgs, John Odom, George Stoll, David Gluck, Elizabeth Coffey, Margie Donnelly, Margie Skidmore, Berenica Cipcus, Iris Burman, Randy Burman, Don Blomberg, Vince Peranio, Bob Adams, Mark Lazarus, David Layman, C. Maloney, Richard Keller, Charlie Swope, Barry Golome, Ed Peranio, Elia Katz, Steve Waters, Billy Davis, Howard Gruber, Van Smith, Chuck Yeaton, Mark Isherwood, Cowboy, and Lawrence Irvine.

Divine's makeup and costumes: Van Smith
Titles: Alan Roso and Randy Burman
Technical assistance: Vince Peranio, Ed Peranio, Barry Golome, Bob Adams
Set design: Vince Peranio
Stills: Lawrence Irvine

Produced, directed, written, and filmed by John Waters

SYNOPSIS: Because of an article in "one of your sleazier national tabloids," Divine, the filthiest person alive, has been forced to go undercover as Babs Johnson. She's living in a trailer in Phoenix, Md., with her traveling companion, Cotton (Mary Vivian Pearce); her delinquent son, Crackers (Danny Mills); and her mentally ill, egg-obsessed mother, Miss Edie (Edith Massey).

Connie and Raymond Marble (Mink Stole and David Lochary) are two jealous perverts who hate Divine because *they* aspire to be the filthiest people alive. They keep two girls, who are impregnated by their servant, Channing (Channing Wilroy), locked in their basement and sell the babies to lesbian couples, investing the profits in a chain of pornography stores. They also front money to heroin pushers working inner-city elementary schools.

The Marbles interview Cookie (Cookie Mueller), who could go for a sandwich. Cookie explains to the Marbles that she can help them dethrone Divine as the filthiest person alive. She confides that she has a date that afternoon with Crackers, and, through that, can learn where Divine is living.

After Cookie has sex with Crackers (and a chicken) in his shack, she calls the Marbles, who are sucking each other's toes and who have Technicolor pubic hair, and tells them where Divine lives. The Marbles send Divine a turd via special delivery.

At her trailer, Divine opens the package, much to Crackers' horror—"Mama, nobody sends you a turd and expects to live!" The enclosed card—"Happy Birthday, Fatso!"—is signed "The filthiest people alive." Divine proclaims that she will out-filth and then kill the assholes who did this.

The next day, the Marbles spy on Divine's birthday party, where she receives gifts of rubber vomit, a meat cleaver, and a pig's head. A snake charmer performs but is upstaged by the Singing Asshole. The Marbles call the authorities; when the police (Bob Adams, other actors) arrive at Divine's party, the partygoers kill and eat them.

In response, Divine and Crackers break into the Marbles' home and lick all their furniture and possessions. They become excited, and Divine gives Crackers a blow job. The pair discover Channing locked in a closet, then find the women in the basement. They untie the girls and allow them to kill Channing.

Elsewhere, the Marbles, believing Divine has been imprisoned, set fire to her trailer, which burns to the ground. Cotton, Crackers, and Divine arrive later to discover an inferno.

When Raymond and Connie return home, their furniture rejects them ("How can a couch be out of order?"). They discover Channing's body and realize the pregnant girls are gone. Much screaming ensues. Divine, Crackers, and Cotton arrive and kidnap the Marbles.

Divine calls a press conference; representatives from *The Tattler, Midnight,* and *Confidential* are in attendance. Crackers explains why this isn't just a publicity stunt, and Cotton talks about happiness. Divine discusses her politics and poses for photographs. She tells the press that she is a lesbian and that blood turns her on.

Divine presides over a kangaroo court. She questions Cotton, then Crackers, then gives the verdict: The Marbles are "guilty of all 10 counts of first-degree stupidity." Divine taunts the Marbles ("Connie Marble, you stand convicted of assholism. The proper punishment will now take place"), then shoots them.

Divine, Crackers, and Cotton decide to move to Boise, Ida., where they will change their appearance—"I think I'll dye my hair another color and start dressing like a dyke!"—and live in gas station toilets. They declare themselves the filthiest people in the world.

Later, on a Baltimore street, Pat Moran's dog evacuates. Divine scoops up the dog turd, eats it, and smiles as Patti Page sings "How Much Is That Doggie In The Window?"

BEST MOMENT: Take your pick.

LOW POINT: Divine gives her son a blow job.

BEST DIALOGUE:
Connie Marble [*rejecting a potential spy*]: You can eat shit for all I care, Miss Sandstone.

Connie Marble [*to the same potential spy*]: I guess there's just two kinds of people, Miss Sandstone: my kind of people and assholes. It's rather obvious which category you fit into. Have a nice day.

Divine: Oh, my God almighty, someone has sent me a bowel movement!

Divine [*while licking the Marbles' furniture*]: This is where they eat, Crackers. This is where they shove dirty little pieces of bacteria down their weaselly little throats. This is where they spread germs, disease, and infection—gobbling obscene fruits and vegetables all in the name of health. How disgusting! Get this table soaking wet!

Cotton [*seeing the trailer burning*]: Oh, no! Our priceless theatrical wardrobe!

Cotton [*to a reporter*]: Murder merely relieves tension, Mr. Kazan. For murder to bring happiness, one must already be happy.

Divine [*to a reporter*]: Kill everyone now! Condone first-degree murder! Advocate cannibalism! Eat shit! Those are my politics!

WHAT TO WATCH FOR: A decorative plate near Edie's crib that reads GOD BLESS OUR MOBILE HOME; Waters' apartment, used as the Marbles' home, has movie posters on the wall that include *The Queen, Boom!* and *Baby Doll*; Mary Vivian Pearce and Danny Mills trying hard not to laugh during the turd-in-the-mail sequence; Mink Stole nearly igniting her fur coat when she sets fire to Divine's trailer; references to the Manson family that appear throughout, such as the Marbles' framed photograph of Susan Atkins and FREE TEX WATSON spray-painted on the side of a building.

WATERSISMS: A long scene with no dialogue, in which Divine drives a souped-up convertible around downtown Baltimore while twangy rock music plays; a long shot of Divine walking through downtown Baltimore while strangers gawk.

DREAMLANDER ALERT: Bob Adams plays the cop who gets shot; Pat Moran's mom is the cashier in the grocery store (which was actually owned by the Morans); the jogger who gets run off the road is Steve Waters, John's brother; and Waters himself provides the voice of the film's narrator, Mr. Jay.

READING MATERIAL ALERT: In a scene excised from the film, Divine reads aloud from *Midnight*.

PRETENTIOUS THEORY ABOUT THIS FILM: The Lady Divine of *Pink Flamingos* is the same Lady Divine of *Multiple Maniacs* and *Mondo Trasho,* previous films in which that same-named character died, which suggests that she is an immortal or otherworldly being who cannot be killed. In the introduction, Mr. Jay discusses the notorious Lady Divine as if we already know who she is and mentions that her recent sleazy press has caused her to "go underground" with an alias. This time out, Lady Divine survives those out to get her, and the character vanishes from Waters' oeuvre, to be replaced hereafter by other fictional characters who prove more fallible.

TRIVIA: The directions to the trailer that David Lochary gives to the police are exactly how one gets to the location. When the Marbles mail Divine a turd, they address it "To: Divine, A trailer, Phoenix, MD; From: The Filthiest People Alive." Cookie

Mueller's newborn son, Max, plays the baby, Noodles. David Lochary and Mink Stole colored their own hair for the film. She used red ink; he used blue Magic Marker. The interiors for the Marble home were actually John Waters' home. He was living there with Mink Stole during the shooting. In 1976, *Pink Flamingos* was featured in the Bicentennial Salute to American Film Comedy at the Museum of Modern Art in New York. The 1997 theatrical rerelease of *Pink Flamingos* grossed over $250,000. The movie is subtitled *An Exercise in Bad Taste*. The original trailer for *Pink Flamingos* features no footage from the film. Instead, scary audience members are interviewed about *Pink Flamingos* as they exit a movie theater. Sound clips from the film are played while quotes from newspaper reviews flash on the screen.

NOTES: The 25th anniversary edition of *Pink Flamingos*, released to theaters and on videocassette, includes a commentary by Waters after the film. He speaks directly to the camera about the making of the film and the scenes he cut before its release. Of the excised footage, these scenes are shown: Edie sits in her playpen in bra and panties, mindlessly introducing eggs to each other ("Freddy, this is JoAnn. JoAnn, this is Freddy") before eating one of them. Divine discusses her capacity for perfection and wanders naked through her trailer. On their way to Divine's trailer, the Marbles hear a bird chirping and complain about the horrors of nature. Raymond wonders "what people would think if they knew that animals were busy shitting and fucking" in the forest. When the Marbles arrive at Divine's trailer, they deliver a rubber tire swing. They tie up Edie, crack eggs on her, put a baby bonnet on her head, and shove toilet paper into her mouth. Divine, Cotton, and Crackers come home and discover Edie. Channing complains to the Marbles about having to fuck girls. Crackers delivers *Midnight* to Divine, who's on the cover. Crackers shows Divine a wanted poster that includes her many aliases, most notably Divine's real name, Glenn Milstead ("Glenn Milstead? I only used that on one day of hanging paper. And look, they've even got 'The Hog Princess' down here!"). Divine and Cotton take naps and Cotton awakens to discover boll weevils in her hair.

Other scenes excised from the film include an entire violent subplot involving Cookie the spy; Pat Moran as Patty Hitler, who tells Divine all the latest gossip, including Cookie's whereabouts; Cotton and Crackers visiting Cookie's home and killing her and her mother, followed by Crackers gargling with Cookie's blood; Cotton and Crackers bringing Divine Cookie's ear, which she eats; Divine and Crackers scoffing at the Marbles' home ("Look at how pissy these turds must be! Touch everything, Crackers! Let our divinity and fame be felt on everything in this middle-class dump!"); Connie ranting about Channing wearing her underwear ("His nipples have actually touched where I have rested mine!"); at the kangaroo court, Divine cutting off Connie's hair; and finally, Divine, Cotton, and Crackers skipping through the forest singing, "We are the filthiest people in the whole wide world" in pig Latin.

WHAT THE CRITICS SAID:
Beyond pornography...the nearest American film to Buñuel's *Andalusian Dog*.

—*New York* magazine

From the grotesque to the hilarious. Really holds your attention.
—*The Village Voice*

Lewd! Shameless! May God forgive its makers for concocting such a vulgar, offensive mess! And may audiences the world over be forever grateful.
—*Philadelphia Daily News*

filthy

What the Truman Capote set is wallowing in these days.

—*Oui*

Proceed immediately...the sickest movie ever made, and one of
the funniest.

—*Interview*

Pink Flamingos certainly does not present any alternative to our
society. The movie ends with Divine eating poodle shit on her way
to Boise, Idaho, and eating poodle shit is not much of an alternative.

—*The Pennsylvania Voice*

Surely one of the most vile, stupid, and repulsive films ever made.

—*Variety*

Like a septic tank explosion, it has to be seen to be believed.

—*Detroit Free Press*

FEMALE TROUBLE

1974, 16 and 35mm color, 92 minutes

A Dreamland Production

Starring Divine, David Lochary, Mary Vivian Pearce, Mink Stole, and Edith Massey as Ida. With Cookie Mueller, Susan Walsh, Michael Potter, Ed Peranio, Paul Swift, George Figgs, Susan Lowe, Channing Wilroy, George Hulse, Betty Woods, Seymour Avigdor, Pat Moran, Chris Mason, Margie Skidmore, Cindy Chosky, Lynn Russo, Elizabeth Coffey, Roland Hertz, Hilary Taylor, Marina Melin, Al Strapelli, Mummy, Berenica Cipcus, Laurel Douglas, and George Stover.

Costume and makeup by Van Smith
Sets by Vincent Peranio
Production chief: Pat Moran
Sound: Bob Maier
Lighting: David Insley
Assistant cameraman: David Insley
Editors: Charles Roggero, John Waters
Production assistance: Cinemen, Steve Yeager
Stills: Bruce Moore, Elaine Jankonus, Mink Stole
Hairstyles: Chris Mason, David Lochary
Special effects: Ed Peranio
Titles: Randy Burman, Alan Rose, with special assistance from Dolores Deluxe

Written, directed, and filmed by John Waters

SYNOPSIS: Poor Dawn Davenport! When she doesn't get cha-cha heels for Christmas, she pulls the Christmas tree down on her mother and leaves home. Dawn (Divine) gets picked up by Earl Peterson (Divine), who takes her to a garbage dump and screws her. Several months later, Dawn gives birth to a baby, whom she names Taffy.

Dawn marries Gator (Michael Potter), a hairdresser at the Lipstick Beauty Salon who lives next door with his Aunt Ida (Edith Massey). The salon's owners, Donald and Donna Dasher (Mary Vivian Pearce and David Lochary), hire Dawn to pose for some unusual photographs of herself performing acts of crime because they view beauty and crime as one. Dawn returns home to find that Taffy (Mink Stole) has covered herself in ketchup and is playing "car accident," her favorite game. Next door, Ida (who hates Dawn and wishes Gator were gay) tries to fix up Gator with her gay pal Ernie (Bob Adams). Gator tells Ida he is moving to Detroit to join the auto industry. Ida has a nervous breakdown.

While the Dashers photograph Dawn at home, Ida barges in and throws acid in Dawn's face. The Dashers visit Dawn, who has been horribly disfigured by the acid, as she recovers in the hospital. They teach her to mainline liquid eyeliner, then force her to model while they photograph her. As a special surprise, they present her with Ida, whom they've kidnapped and placed in a giant birdcage. Dawn chops off Ida's hand with an ax.

Taffy murders her father, then joins the Hare Krishnas. When she visits Dawn backstage at the nightclub where Dawn's about to perform her new act, Dawn strangles her.

Dawn performs her nightclub act, which involves posing while jumping on a trampoline and throwing mackerel at the audience. She shoots several audience members ("Who wants to die for art?") before fleeing.

Police officers discover Dawn living in a tent in the woods. In court, Dawn admits to everything and reminds the jurors that she is "the most famous person you've ever seen! Take notes while you have the chance!"

Dawn is sentenced to die in the electric chair. Before she dies, she reads an acceptance speech and, smiling maniacally, is electrocuted.

BEST MOMENTS: Dawn's trampoline act; Ida pleading with Gator to become a homosexual; Dawn's reaction to the Dashers' mascara brush hors d'oeuvres.

LOW POINTS: Divine (as Earl) shows us his filthy penis; a one-eyed man pops out his glass eye.

BEST DIALOGUE:
Ida [*screaming at Taffy to get her some food*]: I don't want no goddamned eggs. I want meat and potatoes!

Dawn [*complaining about the hardships of motherhood*]: I've done everything a mother can do. I've locked her in her room, I've beaten her with the car aerial, nothing changes her. It's hard being a loving mother. I give her free food, a bed, clean underpants, what does she expect?

Ida to Gator: You could change! Queers are just better. I'd be so proud if you was a fag and had a nice beautician boyfriend…. I worry that you'll work in an office, have children, celebrate wedding anniversaries. The world of a heterosexual is a sick and boring life.

Dawn [*ignoring Taffy's desire to attend school*]: There is no need to know about presidents, wars, numbers, or science.

Taffy [*rebuffing her father's advances*]: I wouldn't suck your lousy dick if I were suffocating and there was oxygen in your balls.

Dawn [*commenting on her daughter's appearance*]: Look in the mirror, Taffy. For 14, you don't look so good.

Dawn [*ending her nightclub act*]: I framed Leslie Bacon! I called the heroin hotline on Abbie Hoffman! I bought the gun that Bremer used to shoot Wallace! I blew Richard Speck! And I'm so fucking beautiful I can't stand it myself!

WHAT TO WATCH FOR: In the garbage dump sex scene, Earl has a racing stripe in his underpants; just before giving birth, Dawn sticks her chewing gum to the wall; during the film's middle section, Dawn is a dead ringer for the young Priscilla Presley; when Divine swims across a stream, she gets carried downstream by the current but continues the scene; in the courtroom scene, Donna Dasher wears a costume based on one worn by the Evil Queen in Disney's *Snow White*; Mr. Wineberger tells Dawn to "start writing" sentences on the board, but it's clear that at least one sentence has already been written on the board; finally, *Female Trouble* contains several references to *Pink Flamingos*, most notably Edie's harangue: "I don't want no goddamned eggs!"

WATERSISMS: Juvenile delinquents; abortion; hairdos; fame; makeup.

DREAMLANDER ALERT: George Stover, with whom Waters attended junior high school, makes his first appearance. He plays the prison chaplain at the end of the film. In the courtroom scene, Mimi Lochary is one of the jurors. Bob Adams plays Ida's queer friend, Ernie. Susan Lowe is Vikki, the receptionist at the Lipstick Beauty Salon; Marina Melin plays Shirl; Channing Wilroy is a lawyer in the courtroom scenes. "And here's a scary one," Waters says. "When Divine whips his dick out in the scene with Taffy, it's actually Chuck Yeaton's cock you see!"

READING MATERIAL ALERT: Dawn reads a scandal sheet called *Secrets*.

PRETENTIOUS THEORY ABOUT THIS FILM: *Female Trouble* is Waters' own rumination on fame in the wake of *Pink Flamingos,* which delivered the success and (better yet) notoriety he had long coveted. Waters knew that any attempt to top the grossness of *Pink Flamingos* was a dead-end street, and after this film and *Desperate Living,* Waters ended the shock/underground phase of his career for good. *Female Trouble* shows what Waters will become: a keen-witted satirist with a unique take on depraved American values.

TRIVIA: The title song is sung by Divine and written by John Waters and Bob Harvey. The scene with Dawn, Concetta, and Chiclet sitting on Dawn's bed is a reference to the infamous *Valley of the Dolls* poster of Patty Duke, Barbara Parkins, and Sharon Tate. The model helicopter shown during the opening titles was made by Tex Watson.

NOTES: There exists a longer cut of *Female Trouble*, known to fans as the "European version" because it was once commercially available overseas from Castle Pictures Video. This version of the film—now available on DVD—includes a lengthy scene in the Dashers' hair salon detailing the breakup of Dawn's marriage; a long interaction between Ida and Taffy; an outtake featuring the Dashers; and lots of comic interplay between the salon's patrons and stylists, including a scene in which the hairdressers "take back" a hairdo from a customer who refuses to pay. Concetta and Chiclet also have more screen time, and the ending credits sequence is longer and backed by Divine singing a ballad version of the title song.

MUSIC USED IN THE MOVIE INCLUDES: "Female Trouble" performed by Divine; "Dig" by Nervous Norvus.

filthy

WHAT THE CRITICS SAID:
Yes, it is ugly. But also fantastic—the frontier of ugliness.

—Oui

Where do these people come from? Where do they go when the sun goes down? Isn't there a law or something?

—Rex Reed

DESPERATE LIVING

1977, 16 and 35mm color, 90 minutes

A Charm City Production

Starring Liz Renay, Mink Stole, Susan Lowe, Edith Massey, Mary Vivian Pearce, and introducing Jean Hill. With Cookie Mueller, Marina Melin, Sharon Niesp, Ed Peranio, Channing Wilroy, George Stover, Turkey Joe, Steve Parker, Peter Koper, Steve Butow, Roland Hertz, H.C. Kliemisch, George Figgs, and George Hulse.

Art director/Set designer: Vincent Peranio
Costumes/makeup: Van Smith
Director of photography: Thomas Loizeaux
Film editor: Charles Roggero
Sound: Robert Maier
Assistant camera: David Insley
Assistant lighting: Kevin Weber
Assistant sound: Richard Ellsberry
Production manager: Pat Moran
Unit manager: Robert Maier
Assistant art director: Dolores Deluxe
Assistant set designers: Steve Parker, Ed Peranio
Special effects: Ed Peranio, Tom Watkins
Credits: Alan Rose
Stills: Steve Yeager, Laurel Douglas
Video: William Platt
Hairdresser: Chris Mason

Assistant makeup: Celeste Hall, Hon Aaron
Music composed by Chris Lobinger
Music arranged by Allen Yarus and Chris Lobinger
Associate producers: William Platt, David Spencer, James McKenzie

Directed, written, and filmed by John Waters

SYNOPSIS: Pity Peggy Gravel! After her housekeeper, Grizelda Brown (Jean Hill), murders Peggy's husband by sitting on his face, the two flee to Mortville, a nearby town where criminals live. They meet Mole McHenry (Susan Lowe), a man trapped in a woman's body, and her live-in girlfriend, Muffy St. Jacques (Liz Renay).

Peggy (Mink Stole) and Grizelda visit the court of Queen Carlotta (Edith Massey), who force-feeds them live cockroaches and demands that they both be given a royal makeover. Princess Coo-Coo (Mary Vivian Pearce) announces her plans to marry Herbert, a garbage collector at the local nudist colony. Carlotta grounds Coo-Coo until her 40th birthday, and sends her officers to murder Herbert.

Mole wins the Baltimore lottery and spends her winnings on a sex change operation. Grizelda is killed during a fight with Carlotta's cops. Coo-Coo is evicted from the palace, and Peggy becomes the new princess. She orders Carlotta's soldiers to spread rabies all over town. When Muffy doesn't like Mole's new penis, Mole cuts it off and throws it into the street, where a dog eats it.

The lesbians storm Carlotta's castle. They kill all the guards, and Coo-Coo bites her mother. Mole kills Peggy, then proclaims Mortville a free city and delivers Carlotta, glazed and covered in canned pineapple, to the citizens. She crowns Muffy the new queen, and as the revelers dance, Coo-Coo expires.

BEST MOMENT: The first several minutes of this film, during which Mink Stole emotes and throws temper tantrums, are absolutely hilarious. Pat Moran's performance as the Bathroom Pervert is also delightful.

LOW POINT: Jean Hill and Mink Stole simulate sex.

BEST DIALOGUE:
Peggy Gravel [*on the phone to a wrong number*]: Hello? What number are you calling? You've dialed the wrong number! Sorry? What good is that? How can you ever repay the 30 seconds you have stolen from my life?

Peggy [*on her way to Mortville*]: I can't stand this scenery another minute! All natural forests should be turned into housing developments! I want cement covering every blade of grass in this nation! Don't we taxpayers have a voice anymore?

Peggy to Mole: I'm a very wealthy woman!
Mole: Yeah? And I'm Cybill Shepherd!

Coo-Coo: Herbert doesn't care if I have ears, he only cares about my mind!

Mole [*at Johns Hopkins demanding a sex change operation*]: Cut the sermons and give me my wang! I want a wang and I want it now!

Queen Carlotta [*spanking Lieutenant Grogan after he performs a striptease*]: This'll teach you to arouse royalty! I hope you didn't leave no pecker tracks on my gown!

WHAT TO WATCH FOR: A nudist on a pogo stick; Liz Renay's breasts appearing through holes in the bathroom wall; Mole struggling to hook Muffy's bra; Turkey Joe flubbing several of his lines.

DREAMLANDER ALERT: Watch for a quick insert of Jean, Edith Massey's roommate, in the scene where Peggy and Grizelda first arrive in Mortville. Chuck Yeaton, Pat Moran's husband, is one of Queen Carlotta's goons.

READING MATERIAL ALERT: Princess Coo-Coo reads a *My Love* comic book.

PRETENTIOUS THEORY ABOUT THIS FILM: The cooked rat imagery of the title credits illustrates the principle that people will swallow anything as long as it's served attractively. It's a convenient metaphor for Waters' entire career, and for show business in general.

TRIVIA: This is not only the first Waters feature film without Divine, but it's also the first to feature an all-original score. It's also the first in which rock and soul music are not featured prominently on the soundtrack.

NOTES: The interiors and exteriors of the Gravel home were shot at Waters' parents' house.

WHAT THE CRITICS SAID:
Desperate Living lingers in the memory as a cautionary fable, told with great passion, wit, and a definite sense of morality.
—*Take One*

Waters' only talent as a director seems to be that he is able to elicit laughter for scenes that under other circumstances would only be appreciated by the kind of people who follow ambulances.
—*Gay Community News*

POLYESTER

1981, 35mm color, 85 minutes

Robert Shaye and Michael White present a John Waters film

Starring Divine and Tab Hunter. With Edith Massey, David
Samson, Mary Garlington, Ken King, Mink Stole, Joni Ruth
White, Hans Kramm, and Stiv Bators as Bo-Bo.

Art director: Vincent Peranio
Costumes and makeup: Van Smith
Editor: Charles Roggero
Assistant director/casting: Pat Moran
Line producer/production manager: Robert Maier
Music: Chris Stein, Michael Kamen
Director of photographer: David Insley
Associate producer: Sara Risher
Executive producer: Robert Shaye

Produced, written, and directed by John Waters

SYNOPSIS: Pitiful Francine Fishpaw (Divine) is distraught. Her
husband, Elmer (David Samson), runs a porno theater and is having an affair with his sleazy secretary, Sandra (Mink Stole).
Francine's daughter, Lu-Lu (Mary Garlington), is pregnant and
wants to have an abortion. Her son, Dexter (Ken King), is the
Baltimore Foot Stomper. Her mother, La Rue (Joni Ruth White),
steals money from Francine's purse and tells her she's fat.
Francine's only friend is heiress Cuddles Kovinsky (Edith

Massey), a former housekeeper who thinks she's a debutante.

Francine takes to drinking. She meets a tall, handsome stranger named Todd Tomorrow (Tab Hunter), and they fall in love. Francine attends an Alcoholics Anonymous meeting, where she is heckled into admitting that she's an alcoholic. Lu-Lu has a miscarriage, and Dexter is thrown in prison.

Todd is not really in love with Francine; he's sleeping with her mother. Together they're plotting Francine's downfall. They plan to have her committed, then drain her bank account and sell her house. Their plan is foiled when Cuddles' chauffeur accidentally smashes them with his car. Francine is reunited with her children, who have been rehabilitated. She sprays Glade air freshener and announces that everything smells so much better now.

BEST MOMENTS: Cuddles arrives at Francine's dressed as a teenager; Francine and Cuddles go shopping for Cuddles' new debutante gown; Elmer and Sandra drive through Francine's neighborhood bellowing insults through a loudspeaker; nuns arrive, chanting "Hail Mary" and looking for Lu-Lu, and Francine shouts, "She's in the living room!"

LOW POINT: Before the titles, an enormously unfunny movie scientist explains the wonders of Odorama.

BEST DIALOGUE:
Elmer [*bellowing insults through a loudspeaker*]: Francine Fishpaw...weighs 300 pounds, and she's an alcoholic! She eats an entire cake at one sitting! You should see her stretch marks!

WHAT TO WATCH FOR: Francine's home is littered with huge Glade Solid Air Fresheners; The movie posters in Elmer's office are from *Faster, Pussycat! Kill! Kill!* and *The Christine Jorgensen Story*; Divine scowls at an empty bottle of scotch in a split-second impersonation of Neely O'Hara in *Valley of the Dolls*; the marquee at the Edmondson advertises "Three Marguerite Duras Films," and the concession commercial promises Beluga caviar, oysters, and champagne, and encourages patrons to "ponder the intellectual meaning of cinema"; Divine's former manager, Bernard Jay, appears as the doorman at the Edmondson (he opens the door for Divine); Waters' friend Dennis Dermody is among the perverts leaving the theater where *My Burning Bush* is playing.

WATERSISMS: Shoplifting, Catholicism, auto-related death, vomit, the Manson family.

DREAMLANDER ALERT: Several delightful Dreamlander cameos include Jean Hill as a church choir member who hijacks a bus; Cookie Mueller as Betty Lalinski, a waitress at the White Coffee Pot restaurant; Mary Vivian Pearce and Sharon Niesp as nuns; Marina Melin and Susan Lowe as Dexter's victims; and Steve Yeager, George Stover, and Pat Moran's husband, Chuck Yeaton, as news reporters. Moran's son Brook Yeaton, George Figgs, and John Waters' brother, Steve, and sister-in-law, Sharon, all appear as picketers.

READING MATERIAL ALERT: Lu-Lu owns a copy of *Farrah's World,* a biography of Farrah Fawcett-Majors.

TRIVIA: The film's assistant art director, Dolores Deluxe, is art director Vince Peranio's wife; she played the Johns Hopkins nurse in *Desperate Living*. Divine's assistant and close friend Jay Bennett is one of the dressers.

NOTES: The title song is written by Deborah Harry, sung by Tab Hunter, produced by Michael Kamen, and performed by members of Harry's group, Blondie. Michael White, who produced *The Rocky Horror Picture Show,* is one of the producers of this film.

WHAT THE CRITICS SAID:
[Waters] negotiates this terrain with the swift assurance of a sea-
soned pilot on a kamikaze mission.

—The Advocate

Tab Hunter and Divine's love scenes are inoffensively depraved,
all part of Waters' pungent satire of an America gone mad.

—People

Camp followers may enjoy Divine's eye-rolling reactions, but to
the uninitiated, most scenes play as overacted melodrama.

—Variety

Tacky, tacky, tacky…but for any suitably depraved moviegoer, it
offers as many honest laughs as *Airplane!* It's a vision of Baltimore
that H.L. Mencken might have loved.

—Time

HAIRSPRAY

1988, 35mm color, 90 minutes

New Line Cinema presents, in association with Stanley F. Buchtal, a Robert Shaye production, a John Waters film

Starring Sonny Bono, Ruth Brown, Divine, Debbie Harry, Ricki Lake, and Jerry Stiller. Featuring Colleen Fitzpatrick, Michael St. Gerard, Leslie Ann Powers, Clayton Prince, Mink Stole, and Shawn Thompson. Special appearances by Ric Ocasek and Pia Zadora.

Choreographer: Edward Love
Casting director: Mary Colquhoun
Casting director, Baltimore: Pat Moran
Art director: Vincent Peranio
Costume and makeup design: Van Smith
Hair design: Christine Mason
Line producer: Robert Maier
Edited by Janice Hampton
Director of photography: David Insley
Coproducers: Stanley Buchtal, John Waters
Executive producers: Robert Shaye, Sara Risher
Producer: Rachel Talalay

Written and directed by John Waters

SYNOPSIS: Tracy Turnblad (Ricki Lake) and Penny Pingleton (Leslie Ann Powers) love *The Corny Collins Show,* a local teen dance music program. Tracy's mother, Edna Turnblad (Divine), doesn't. She thinks it isn't right, kids dancing on TV to "colored music."

Tracy aces an audition for *The Corny Collins Show*. She steals *Corny Collins* star Amber Von Tussle's (Colleen Fitzpatrick) boyfriend, Link (Michael St. Gerard). Tracy is against segregation on *Corny Collins,* which may hurt her in the Miss Auto Show competition. Station manager Arvin Hodgepile (Divine) threatens to cancel Corny's show if one colored kid ends up on camera. Tracy is busted at a race riot and taken to reform school.

At the Auto Show, Mr. Von Tussle (Sonny Bono) plants a time bomb in Mrs. Von Tussle's (Deborah Harry) wig, and tells her that if Amber loses, Mrs. Von Tussle should throw the bomb. On *The Corny Collins Show,* Tracy is announced as the winner of Miss Auto Show, but because she's is in reform school, the title goes to Amber.

Tracy is freed from reform school and arrives just in time to accept her crown. She hollers, "Let's dance!"

BEST MOMENT: The *Corny Collins* kids perform the Madison.

LOW POINT: Mrs. Von Tussle dons rubber gloves and pops Amber's zit.

BEST DIALOGUE:
Mr. Pinky [*in a commercial for the Hefty Hideaway*]: Are you big-boned, got a glandular problem, but still want the glamour?

Tracy to Link: I wish…I wish I was dark-skinned!
Link: Tracy, our *souls* are black, even though our skin is white.

Beatnik chick (Pia Zadora): I play my bongos, listen to Odetta, then I iron my hair. Dig?… When I'm high, I *am* Odetta!… Let's get naked and smoke!

WHAT TO WATCH FOR: A scary framed photo of a young Mr. and Mrs. Turnblad in their home; at the Von Tussles', the subject of the faux Walter Keane painting has the same hairdo as Debbie Harry; Amber has a photo of Steve Lawrence on her vanity mirror; a rat scurries through a mud puddle reflecting the moon; at the final protest, one of the picket signs reads, "Amber is an asshole."

WATERSISMS: A girl vomits on an amusement park ride.

DREAMLANDER ALERT: Mary Vivian Pearce is the mother of a hair hopper; Susan Lowe is an angry mom; George Stover plays a policeman; Chuck Yeaton is a newsman, and his son Brook plays "Tough Guy #1"; Rosemary Knower is Mrs. Shipley, the special ed teacher; Doug Roberts is Penny's dad; David Samson appears as a grouchy TV station manager; Alan Wendl plays Mr. Pinky; and, of course, Waters himself plays the demented Dr. Frederickson.

READING MATERIAL ALERT: In line for *The Corny Collins Show*, Penny reads *Black Like Me*.

TRIVIA: Buddy Deane, on whose TV program *The Corny Collins Show* is based, appears as a television reporter. Dreamlander Channing Wilroy was one of the regulars on *The Buddy Deane Show*. Tilted Acres is based on Gwynn Oak Amusement Park in Baltimore County, where racial problems occurred in the early 1960s. "The Dirty Boogie," which the kids do in Motor Mouth Mabel's record shop, is actually the Bodie Green, the dance that Mary Vivian Pearce does at the end of *Hag in a Black Leather Jacket*.

MUSIC INCLUDES: "Pony Time," "The Fly," "Let's Twist Again," "Limbo Rock," and "Dancing Party" by Chubby Checker;

"Mashed Potato Time" by Dee Dee Sharp; "The Duke of Earl" by Gene Chandler; "Gravy" by Dee Dee Sharp; "Do the New Continental" by the Dovells.

WHAT THE CRITICS SAID:
It seems inappropriate to call ick *noir* auteur Waters a breath of fresh air. But, amid the stale odor of our man-made, musty, Muzaked lives, he's a welcome gust of Renuzit.
—*The Washington Post*

If there is a message in the movie, it is that Waters, who could never in a million years have made the Council, did, after all, survive to make the movie.
—Roger Ebert, *Chicago Sun-Times*

John Waters may never win an Academy Award, which is a shame, because he deserves one, if only for bringing Divine to a mass audience. With one look of motherly love, Divine gives more subtext than any close-up since Garbo.
—*Manhattan GX*

CRY-BABY

1990, 35mm color, 85 minutes

Universal Pictures and Imagine Entertainment present a John Waters film

Starring Johnny Depp, Amy Locane, Susan Tyrrell, Iggy Pop, Ricki Lake, Traci Lords, Stephen Mailer, Darren E. Burrows, Kim McGuire, and Polly Bergen as Mrs. Vernon-Williams. Featuring Patricia Hearst, David Nelson, Troy Donahue, Mink Stole, Joe Dallesandro, Joey Heatherton, and Willem Dafoe.

Casting by Paula Herold, Pat Moran
Music supervised by Becky Mancuso, Tim Sexton
Music score composed by Patrick Williams
Choreographed by Lori Eastside
Hair design by Christine Mason
Wardrobe and makeup designed by Van Smith
Unit production manager: Karen Koch
First assistant director: Mary Ellen Woods
Second assistant director: Jeffrey Wetzel
Production designed by Vincent Peranio
Edited by Janice Hampton
Director of photography: David Insley
Executive producers: Jim Abrahams, Brian Grazer
Producer: Rachel Talalay

Written and directed by John Waters

SYNOPSIS: Goody-goody Allison Vernon-Williams (Amy Locane) is so tired of being good. She wants to date Cry-Baby, a hood who belongs to a gang known as the Drapes. Allison's grandmother, fancy society matron Mrs. Vernon-Williams (Polly Bergen), doesn't approve.

Neither does Allison's square boyfriend, Baldwin (Stephen Mailer). But Allison longs to cavort at Turkey Point Swim Club, a juke joint and swimming hole operated by Cry-Baby and Pepper's grandmother, Ramona Rickettes (Susan Tyrrell) and her boyfriend, Belvedere (Iggy Pop).

At Mrs. Vernon-Williams' charm school, Baldwin and Cry-Baby fight, and Allison rides off on Cry-Baby's bike. At Turkey Point, Pepper gives Allison a bad-girl makeover, and she and Cry-Baby perform "King Cry-Baby," a song about his life as a misunderstood JD.

Later, Cry-Baby explains that his father was the Alphabet Bomber, a maniac who blew up local buildings in alphabetical order (the airport, a barber shop, a car wash, a drugstore...). Cry-Baby's parents were apprehended and sentenced to death by electrocution. Therefore he must do something rotten every day in their honor and cry a single tear.

After a rumble between the Drapes and the Squares, the Judge (Robert Walsh) sentences Cry-Baby to the Maryland Training School for Boys until his 21st birthday. He's eventually pardoned, just in time to rescue Allison from the Squares and a certain life of boredom. Everyone cries a single tear, except Cry-Baby and Alison, who both cry two tears—one out of each eye.

BEST MOMENTS: Mink Stole arrives in an iron lung. Wanda's parents discuss the meaning of the word "fuck." At the Chatterbox Orphanage, children are put on display like merchandise.

LOW POINTS: A rat laughs at Cry-Baby. Hatchet-Face scares a cow.

BEST DIALOGUE:
Mrs. Wood: What does "fuck" mean, Hector?
Mr. Wood: Oh, Meg, it's just a teen nonsense word Wanda uses to make herself feel all grown-up.
Mrs. Wood [*to judge*]: Your honor, may we take Wanda the fuck home?

Baldwin to Cry-Baby: You crybaby, you!
Cry-Baby: That's *Mister* Baby to you!

Mrs. Wood: "Let's all put on a folk hat and learn something about a foreign culture!"

WHAT TO WATCH FOR: Cry-Baby gets a prison tattoo of a teardrop under his eye, but it's gone by the time of the press conference; in the jailbreak sequence, Hatchet-Face is dressed as the Evil Queen from Disney's *Snow White*; Cry-Baby's car radio works even when the car isn't running.

WATERSISMS: Rats; a woman delivers her own baby; reform school.

DREAMLANDER ALERT: Susan Lowe is among the parents in the night-court sequence; Mary Vivian Pearce appears for a brief second as a woman playing cards at Turkey Point; Alan J. Wendl is Toe Joe Jackson.

READING MATERIAL ALERT: Milton Hackett reads a comic book titled *Tales to Astonish*.

PRETENTIOUS THEORY ABOUT THIS FILM: With the scene where the 3-D movie is shown to prison inmates, Waters presents the concept of art as an attack on a captive audience. By having Hatchet-Face crash through the screen and terrify the prisoners,

Waters introduces his old theme of terrorizing an unsuspecting audience. The prisoners here are stand-ins for the unwary children who sat through Waters' childhood puppet shows.

TRIVIA: "The Four B's" that Mrs. Vernon-Williams recites are borrowed from Waters' grandmother Stella Whitaker, who used to espouse the same beliefs. Both "crybaby" and "hatchet-face" are terms used to describe Peggy Gravel in *Desperate Living*. When Allison sings, Amy Locane is lip-synching to recordings by the wonderful Rachel Sweet. The story is set in 1954, but "Cry-Baby" by the Bonnie Sisters, the song that opens the film, wasn't a hit until 1956. (Waters uses a remake by three unrelated session singers who call themselves "The Honey Sisters.") Furthermore, Milton Hackett is seen reading a copy of Marvel Comics' *Tales To Astonish,* a title that wasn't published until 1959. Although most fans point to *Cry-Baby* as their least favorite Waters film, it's the only one of his movies other than *Hairspray* to get a good review out of Roger Ebert. And Waters says, "*Cry-Baby* is by far the most-seen of my movies, because it's on TV *constantly!*"

About the distinctly different version of *Cry-Baby* that airs on cable television's USA Network, Waters told the author, "They cut out all the good stuff, and then it had to be 80 minutes long for TV, so they padded it with footage that had been cut from the original version."

NOTES: Actor Stephen Mailer is Norman Mailer's son. The old Universal logo is revived for this film—actually one that was retired long before the 1950s: the version with the biplane circling the globe, which dates back to the 1930s.

WHAT THE CRITICS SAID:
Cry-Baby is a good many things, including a passable imitation of a 1950s teenage exploitation movie.
—Roger Ebert, *Chicago Sun-Times*

Not so much a lampoon as a celebration of clichés, *Cry-Baby* has less to say about adolescence and learning to be one's own person than 1988's *Hairspray*. And some of (Waters') notions—racial harmony among the blacks and rednecks of the period, for instance—seem especially thin coming from the maker of *Pink Flamingos*. While this is a common conceit among the makers of nerd vengeance comedies, surely Waters is capable of something a tad more original.

—Rita Kempley, *The Washington Post*

Instead of building a complete movie story around Depp, Waters seems to have instead taken one *Hairspray* element, a skit revolving around "bad kids" vs. "good kids," if you will, and stretched it to feature-length by padding the film with redundant jokes.

—Chris Hicks, *Deseret News*

SERIAL MOM

1994, 35 mm color, 93 minutes

A Savoy Pictures presentation of a Polar Entertainment Production; A Film by John Waters

Starring Kathleen Turner, Sam Waterston, Ricki Lake, Matthew Lillard, Mary Jo Catlett, Justin Whalin, Patricia Dunnock, Mink Stole, Patricia Hearst, and Suzanne Somers.

Music by Basil Poledouris
Music supervisor: Bones Howe
Casting by Paula Herold and Pat Moran
Costumes by Van Smith
Production designer: Vincent Peranio
Edited by Janice Hampton and Erica Huggins
Director of photography: Robert M. Stevens, A.S.C.
Executive producer: Joseph Caracciolo, Jr.
Produced by John Fiedler and Mark Tarlov

Written and directed by John Waters

SYNOPSIS: Beverly Sutphin (Kathleen Turner) is the perfect wife and mom. So what if she kills people who piss her off? Her husband Eugene (Sam Waterston), son, Chip (Matthew Lillard), and daughter, Misty (Ricki Lake), aren't thrilled with Beverly's hobby. Neither is the Sutphins' neighbor, Dottie Hinkle (Mink Stole). Detectives Pike and Gracey (Scott Morgan, Walt McPherson) aren't exactly delighted either.

Those who are least happy about Beverly's short fuse are her victims, who include Chip's math teacher, Mr. Stubbins (John Badila); neighbors Ralph and Betty Sterner (Kathy Fannon and Doug Roberts); Mrs. Emily Jenson (Patsy Grady Abrams); and Juror #8 (Patricia Hearst) at Beverly's trial. But Beverly is acquitted of their murders and agrees to let Suzanne Somers play her in the TV movie of her life.

BEST MOMENTS: Kathleen Turner makes obscene phone calls to Mink Stole. Stopped at a traffic light, Beverly smiles at a family in the next car; they scream and drive off.

LOW POINTS: Close-up of a dentist's drill. The car chase.

BEST DIALOGUE:
Joan Rivers [*to a talk-show guest*]: I just don't get it. How can you love a mass murderer?
Talk-show guest: Easy. He's handsome, he's famous, and we get conjugal visits.

Misty: Chip, our mother is Charles Manson!

WHAT TO WATCH FOR: Chip's room is decorated with stills from Herschell Gordon Lewis films and posters from *Blood Feast* (1963) and other slasher movies; Misty sells a thrift-store painting of Don Knotts, whom Waters thinks he resembles; a sign outside the local church announcing the day's sermon, "Capital Punishment and You"; Brigid Berlin, Waters' favorite Warhol Factory actress, appears in a brief cameo outside the courtroom.

WATERSISMS: Rats; obsession with slasher films; murder trial groupies—"Didn't I see you at Hinckley?"

DREAMLANDER ALERT: Susan Lowe and Rosemary Knower appear as trial groupies; Mary Vivian Pearce buys a book; John Waters provides the voice of Ted Bundy on Beverly's audio tape; cutie-pie Scott Morgan makes his first Dreamland appearance (he also appears in *Pecker* and *Cecil B. Demented*), as does Tim Caggiano; Alan Wendl is trashman Sloppy; Doug Roberts plays Ralph Sterner; and Warhol superstar Brigid Berlin makes her second appearance in a Waters film.

READING MATERIAL ALERT: Beverly Sutphin owns several true-crime books, among them *Helter Skelter,* and her nighttime reading is usually a study of famous serial murderers.

TRIVIA: The high school used in this film is the same school Divine attended.

NOTES: The song "Gas Chamber" is written by L7 and John Waters. The sequence where Beverly murders the Sterners is an homage to a pair of humdingers: William Castle's *Strait-Jacket* and the Bette Davis creep-out *Hush...Hush, Sweet Charlotte* (1964).

WHAT THE CRITICS SAID:
I am not sure why this isn't very funny, but it's not.
—Roger Ebert, *Chicago Sun-Times*

John Waters' latest, and one of his best, is like an early '60s TV sitcom that keeps lunging into profane naughtiness. Waters builds our disbelief of shows like *Leave It to Beaver* and *Ozzie and Harriet* right into the movie.
—*Los Angeles Times*

Serial Mom is a failed satire.... While the idea sounds fertile, the execution is uneven, and the comedy sporadic at best.
—*Reel Views*

With *Serial Mom,* the renegade director/writer kicks the nation smack in its collective groin, marvelously mocking the oh-so-current mania over crime figures and tabloid scandals.... For those who take their comedy black, this is a high Waters mark.

—*USA Today*

Waters' spiffy new farce...is a tatty freak show.

—*Time*

PECKER

1998, 35mm color, 86 minutes

Fine Line Features presents a Polar Entertainment Production; A Film by John Waters

Starring Edward Furlong, Christina Ricci, Bess Armstrong, Mark Joy, Mary Kay Place, Martha Plimpton, Brendan Sexton III, Mink Stole, and Lili Taylor. With Patricia Hearst and Jean Schertler.

Music by Stewart Copeland
Casting by Pat Moran, Billy Hopkins, Suzanne Smith, and Kerry Barden
Costumes: Van Smith
Production designer: Vincent Peranio
Edited by Janice Hampton, A.S.C.
Director of photography: Robert Stevens, A.S.C.
Executive producers: Mark Ordesky, Jonathan Weisgal, Joe Revitte, Joe Caracciolo Jr.
Produced by John Fiedler and Mark Tarlov

Written and directed by John Waters

SYNOPSIS: Pecker (Edward Furlong), a young photographer, becomes a sensation. His photographs of naughty bits of Baltimore capture the attention of the New York art world after art dealer Rorey Wheeler (Lili Taylor) offers Pecker a show in her Manhattan gallery—much to the horror of his best friend, Matt (Brendan Sexton III), and girlfriend Shelly (Christina Ricci), who runs a

Laundromat. On the other hand, his family—mother Joyce (Mary Kay Place), father Jimmy (Mark Joy), and sugar-addicted sister Little Chrissy (Lauren Hulsey)—are happy about Pecker's new success. Pecker's grandmother Memama (Jean Schertler), who sells drive-through pit beef sandwiches and travels with a miraculous talking plastic Virgin Mary statue, and older sister, Tina (Martha Plimpton), who works in a gay bar, are also happy for Pecker.

After his New York show is a success, Pecker and his family are famous, but his fame changes everything and practically no one is happy about it. Child Protective Services have placed Little Chrissy on Ritalin, and she's now a zombie. Memama's plastic Virgin has stopped speaking. And after middle-class straight people show up at local gay bar the Fudge Palace to see the teabagging they've read about in *City Paper*'s story "Teabaggin' With Pecker," owner Mr. Nellbox fires Tina.

Pecker tells Rorey to cancel his upcoming show at the Whitney. He wants his friends, his family, and his life back. Pecker stages a new show in Baltimore, featuring his photographs of New York art mavens looking stupid. Soon the New York art types are partying with the sleazy Baltimoreans. Mary speaks, this time for real. Little Chrissy, now a vegetarian, snorts peas. The partygoers toast the end of irony, and Pecker says he's thinking of directing a movie.

BEST MOMENTS: Mary speaks. Dad asks Red if it's legal to show pubic hair in New York. Cindy Sherman offers Little Chrissy a Valium.

LOW POINT: A gratuitous beaver shot.

BEST DIALOGUE:
Memama: Sometimes there's things more important than pit beef.

Mary Vivian Pearce on male go-go dancers: Those homos! There's nothing *gay* about it!

Tina to a sniffy art dealer: I work in a gay bar in Baltimore, we call everybody Mary. You've got a little sugar in ya, don't ya? Sure, I can tell. A little light in the loafers. Oh, I don't mean nothin', I love fags!

Memama to Mary: Speak, goddamn it!

Mr. Nellbox [*turning away straight people from his nightclub*]: I need to see some gay ID or you're outta here.

WHAT TO WATCH FOR: "Written and directed by John Waters" appears over the image of two rats screwing in a garbage can. Joyce has Barbie styling heads (a Waters favorite) for sale in her thrift store. In the opening scene, the number of the bus is 7734—an old Catholic school joke (7734 upside down spells hell).

WATERSISMS: Rats, lesbians, strippers, junkies.

DREAMLANDER ALERT: Alan J. Wendl is Mr. Nellbox; Sharon Niesp plays the Pelt Room's bouncer; Mary Vivian Pearce orders a macaroni salad at the Sub Stop; Susan Lowe plays a hairstylist in the Greg Gorman scenes; Channing Wilroy appears as a wise-guy neighbor; Tim Caggiano is Lester; Scott Morgan is Jed; Doug Roberts and Patsy Grady Adams are Dave's parents; Brigid Berlin drops by as "Supermarket Rich Lady"; and John Waters provides the voice of the obscene phone caller—"Put your vagina up to the phone!"

READING MATERIAL ALERT: An obese woman is shown reading a copy of *Fat and Furious*.

PRETENTIOUS THEORY ABOUT THIS FILM: Waters is exploring the process by which photography, a technology that allows any idiot to produce an image worthy of Da Vinci, can make artists of us all. As superaesthete Andy Warhol once said,

"Everything is pretty through the camera's lens." Pecker himself is a Warholian joke, a personification of the camera's innocent gaze and its capacity to spin straw into gold. Waters' final commentary is that any sucker can make art, but it takes someone with real vision to turn the artist into a commodity.

NOTES: Waters co-wrote the songs "Straight Boys" and "Don't Drop the Soap" with Stewart Copeland.

WHAT THE CRITICS SAID:
Nothing the filmmaker has done since 1988's *Hairspray* has clicked and, as sweet as *Pecker* is, it's flimsy whimsy. At least one mystery is finally solved. The length of John Waters' *Pecker?* Blessedly brief at 87 minutes.

—*USA Today*

Waters gives us a young hero who shows better personal judgment than the executive at the center of Monicagate. As comedy, homily, and apologia, this is a treat for adventuresome moviegoers.

—*The Detroit News*

Pecker is…wickedly funny and contains a jolt or two, but nothing on the level of *Pink Flamingos* (1972). Instead, we get a touching and genuinely amusing look at an eccentric group of characters and their crazy world. For once, we aren't laughing at them per se, but with them.

—*Film Threat*

It may, at long last, be time for this filmmaker to turn in his leopard-skin megaphone. Watching *Pecker,* his rickety new comedy about a teenage Baltimore shutterbug, it becomes clear that Waters has grown color-blind to his own sleazo-shock aesthetic.

—*Entertainment Weekly*

Great title, pale film. Go and rent *Female Trouble* again for a real
Waters fix.

—*Film Journal International*

A Disney film for perverts.

—*The Japan Times*

The film is never truly funny, but it's an amusing novelty, gaining
strength from smart characterizations and sly cogency about the
way people are exploited under the limelight of celebrity.

—*San Francisco Chronicle*

CECIL B. DEMENTED

2000, 35mm color, 88 minutes

Artisan Entertainment presents, in association with Le Studio Canal Plus, a Polar Entertainment Production, a John Waters Film

Starring Melanie Griffith, Stephen Dorff, Alicia Witt, Adrian Grenier, Larry Gilliard, Jr., Maggie Gyllenhaal, Jack Noseworthy, Mink Stole, Ricki Lake, Patricia Hearst, Mike Shannon, and Kevin Nealon.

Casting by Pat Moran, C.S.A., and Billy Hopkins, Suzanne Smith, and Kerry Barden
Executive music producer: Christopher Brooks
Music by Zoe Poledouris and Basil Poledouris
Costume designer: Van Smith
Edited by Jeffrey Wolf, A.C.E.
Production designer: Vincent Peranio
Director of Photography: Robert Stevens, A.S.C.
Executive producers: Anthony DeLorenzo, Fred Bernstein
Produced by Joe Caracciolo, Jr., John Fiedler, Mark Tarlov

Written and directed by John Waters

SYNOPSIS: At the Baltimore opening of her new movie, *Some Kind of Happiness,* movie star Honey Whitlock (Melanie Griffith) is kidnapped by Cecil B. Demented (Stephen Dorff) and the Sprocket Holes, a group of obsessed cinema terrorists who object to the state of mainstream movies. During the kidnapping, socialite Sylvia Mallory (Mink Stole) dies of a heart attack.

After his crew gives Honey an ugly makeover, Cecil forces her to star in his no-budget movie, *Raving Beauty*, most of which is shot on location during actual terrorist attacks on the commercial film industry. After the Sprocket Holes (who are each tattooed with the name of their favorite film director) bomb a screening of the director's cut of *Patch Adams*, the news media praise Honey's "performance," and she begins to enjoy her place in Cecil's camp.

The Sprocket Holes attend a Honey Whitlock look-alike contest at a local drive-in (first prize: a 10-pound ham), where Cecil shoots his film's final scene. He asks Honey to set fire to her hair as the Baltimore city police arrive. Most of the Sprocket Holes are arrested or killed, and Cecil saves Honey from police gunfire by setting fire to himself and knocking over a cop who's about to shoot her. As Cecil burns to death, Honey is taken into custody while Liberace sings "Ciao."

BEST MOMENTS: Roseanne interviews Honey Whitlock's ex-husband, played by Eric Roberts. Mary Vivian Pearce pelts Cecil with Good & Plentys.

LOW POINT: To prove their allegiance to Cecil, the Sprocket Holes are branded with Cecil's name.

WHAT TO WATCH FOR: At Cecil's hideout, movie posters are displayed for Otto Preminger's *Carmen Jones* (1954), underground action drama *The Peace Killers* (1971), and blaxploitation flick *Melinda* (1972).

BEST DIALOGUE:
Honey [*after being sent a white limousine*]: Do I look like Liberace's goddamned boyfriend, for chrissake? I have "black limousine only" in my contract.

Cecil to Honey: One day you'll thank me for saving you from your bad career.

Cherish to a Hollywood executive, just before she shoots him: Didn't you just green-light another film based on a video game?

WATERSISMS: Vomit; drive-in theaters; pornography; references to Herschell Gordon Lewis, William Castle, and Kenneth Anger; Honey Whitlock's "ugly makeover"; movie houses that have been turned into churches and bingo halls (a pet peeve of Waters').

DREAMLANDER ALERT: Mink Stole as Sylvia Mallory; Ricki Lake as Libby, Honey Whitlock's assistant; Scott Morgan as Honey's biggest fan; Mary Vivian Pearce, Susan Lowe, and Patsy Grady Abrams as angry moviegoers; Joyce Flick Wendl as a puking woman; Alan J. Wendl as a teamster; Channing Wilroy as a shop steward; Tim Caggiano as a porno fan; Judith Knight Young as the drive-in ticket clerk; Patricia Hearst and Mark Joy as Fidget's parents; Rosemary Knower and Doug Roberts as Cecil's parents; Tyler Miller as a Cecil fan.

READING MATERIAL ALERT: The teamsters at *Gump Again* are reading *Daily Variety*, one of John Waters' favorite magazines.

TRIVIA: The scene in which Cecil asks Honey to set her hair on fire is an homage to Waters' same request of Mink Stole during *Pink Flamingos*.

WHAT THE CRITICS SAID:
The movie has a radical premise...but pitches it at the level of a very bad sketch on *Saturday Night Live*.
—Roger Ebert, Chicago Sun-Times

The film has a giddy silliness that's thoroughly endearing...the actors are a hoot.

—Steve Simels, *TV Guide*

This very personal Waters production, like the guerrilla cineastes it depicts, displays a laughable lack of craftsmanship.

—Bob Strauss, *Los Angeles Daily News*

Consistently amusing and smart in its choice of targets, but it lacks the manic edge of some of Waters' earlier movies.

—Stephen Holden, *The New York Times*

Waters' outlaw analyses of pop culture, always a crucial part of his films, have now started to consume them.

—Owen Gleiberman, *Entertainment Weekly*

Although no masterpiece, it tackles Hollywood on its own ground and scores points through its outlandish satire. At least this cheap, unassuming comedy gives us something to think about. That's more than many studio movies can claim at the moment.

—*The Christian Science Monitor*

Yes, it celebrates guerrilla-style filmmaking, but it's also an uproarious, smartly crafted, hard action flick with a certified Hollywood star, Melanie Griffith.

—*Los Angeles Times*